Crossings 44

LIVERY STABLE BLUES

LIVERY STABLE BLUES

*Nick LaRocca, the Original Dixieland Jazz Band,
And the First Jazz Recording*

Salvatore Mugno

translated by Carlo Massimo

BORDIGHERA PRESS

Published by Bordighera Press, an imprint of the John D. Calandra Italian American Institute of Queens College, The City University of New York.

25 West 43rd Street, 17th Floor, New York, NY 10036

Library of Congress Control Number: 2025942206

The Italian language original *Il biografo di Nick LaRocca* was published by Arcana in 2017.

The cover is an adaptation of the 1917 sheet music cover, Leo Feist, Inc., New York.

© 2017, Salvatore Mugno
© 2025, Carlo Massimo, English translation

Crossings 44
ISBN 978-1-59954-235-5

TABLE OF CONTENTS

CHAPTER ONE

Harry and Nick (April-May 1960)

The year 1960, in spite of everything, turned out to be the climax of Harry Brass' life. The story of Nick LaRocca and his jazz band, at which Brass had slaved away for 23 years, was finished, published, sold here and there, widely panned and mostly ignored.

On the 25th of April Brass had returned in triumph to New Orleans, where he expected to be fêted by his protagonist. He expected to enjoy ten days of attention from the press, too—and, more importantly, a glorious ten-night haze in the nightclubs and sporting houses of the French Quarter.

Crescent City seemed to welcome him as he touched down. The new airport was, to his eyes, the happiest and most elegant in the country, and the mosaics in the pavement made sweet, musical patterns underfoot. His flight from Atlanta, on a well-mannered Viscount plane, arrived at dawn. It gave him just enough time to enjoy the sight of the sleepy, languid working girls coming home from the bars.

He got Room 960 at the Hotel Monteleone: seven dollars a night, with air conditioning and stationary on the desk.

Brass had never felt so happy. Down the street, at Sloppy Joe's, he asked for an Herbsaint frappe.

The shops were just opening when he left. He had his breakfast at Brennan's, looking out on the flowers in its elegant courtyard. He had the eggs Hussarde and two more glasses of Herbsaint, staring in wonder at the crumbs of French bread on the immaculate white tablecloth.

Later Brass made some phone calls to local reporters—TV and print—to see who was interested in interviewing him about his book. Then he took the streetcar down St. Charles Avenue to Jackson, and from there to Constance Street, off Magazine, to the house of a certain cornetist, who was waiting for him.

It was the first they'd met since the book came out.

He wrote me every day that last year; his wife told me later our conversations were what was keeping him alive. Sometimes he was horrible, completely impossible; he was afraid I might be conning him somehow. It all depended on how his heart was doing that day. He had a leaky valve, the same thing I would have 40 years later.

The old musician had shuffled out to the streetcar stop to welcome him. He had the fierce, bewildered gaze of a man ignoring medical advice. He'd lost weight, but wasn't weak; as they walked, he would occasionally kick the pickets of fences he'd built himself, as if to demonstrate their solidity to his young biographer.

Of course he started in right away insulting me, saying the book was superficial, that it was full of mistakes (all of them my fault, obviously, not his)—including the date that America entered World War I! It wasn't April 15, he said, it was the sixth . . .

And so began the decade of glory in the life of Harry Brass.

CHAPTER TWO

Harry (1937-1945)

Harry wasn't quite 18 when he sat in the dark of his school auditorium to watch that projection of *March of Time*. Louis de Rochemont, with some artistic license, had recreated the story of the Original Dixieland Jazz Band. This episode was called "The Birth of Swing."

What an honor it would be, to be Nick's alter ego.

That day twisted the flow of Harry's life; or perhaps it straightened it out. "The Birth of Swing," episode seven, volume three, released February 17, 1937. They had even gotten some of the original members of the ODJB to play themselves.

LaRocca was the glue holding the group together: he'd gone from New Orleans to New York in 1936 to convince his old bandmates, one by one, to get back together. Twenty years had passed since they'd broken up. Now one worked in a bible society, another as a mechanic, another at the YMCA, the fourth in radio.

Larry Shields, the clarinetist, had gray hair now. They tried to cover it up. Henry Ragas, the pianist, was dead; Russel Robinson was standing in for him.

Finally the boys played. Nick gave the order for the mutes to come out, and he gave new life to Larry Shields' old solo in "Tiger Rag" . . .

Twenty rapturous, devastating minutes in dixieland, for Harry.

It wasn't easy being his friend.

In Harry's diary, however, the conversion to dixieland appears on July 7, 1937. It was the day he'd bought and listened to, for the first time, some records of the ODJB. They were Victor 78s, from 1936.

That was the morning that Harry, barely 18, had gotten his driver's license. In other words, it was the date that would decide the rest of his life—not that Harry realized it. He'd gone downtown with his mother that day, who had her own errands. But Harry's destination was Denton, Cotter & Daniels, the biggest record shop in Buffalo. There he asked for the latest from the ODJB.

There were three records out, each with six tracks, but the Denton's only had two available. Mrs. Brass, amused, tapped her toe when the clerk played one for Harry. She had studied the piano and even sang, though only in church. A puritan upbringing kept her far away from jazz, but she'd liked ragtime as a girl and had a small collection of it in sheet music. Many nights, Harry remembered, he and his siblings would sit with her at the piano while she played for them. His father would generally withdraw from these little parties, hunched over his business files and bank documents.

Harry bought the records and ordered the third. That summer he played them constantly, back to back. At the second hand stores he dug through the records, looking for ODJB's old 78s.

I can't tell you how much I admired him.

When school opened at Amherst Central High, Harry was ready to start a dixieland group of his own. He started on the drums. He moved on to the trombone, a Christmas present from his parents, which he played with the confident, honking roar of an autodidact.

In October 1938, Harry decided to write Nick LaRocca. He used his father's business stationary, which conferred a certain solemnity on the letter.

"Maybe I can sell him a car," his father laughed.

The point of the letter was to propose a history of the band, told from the cornetist's point of view. LaRocca wrote back, full of reserve and hesitation.

I was electrified by that letter.

Nothing remains of the pre-War correspondence between Harry and the leader of the ODJB. While Harry was away in the Army, fighting at Normandy and the Bulge, his father made sure to cut off this boyhood obsession to the best he could. Quietly, he sent back LaRocca's letters unopened, one after the other. Eventually they stopped coming.

It was only in 1961 that Harry could recover any of his own letters, and only one of them: the second in an interminable series, dated November 12, 1938. LaRocca himself gave it back to him. In fact he shook it in his face, shouting about the careless promises it contained and threatening a lawsuit for his share of any royalties from the biography. Harry hadn't seen it in 23 years.

"ESTABLISHED 1882—BRASS' CARRIAGE MANUFACTURING CO.," he read. "BUFFALO, NEW YORK—AUTOMOBILE BODIES—MAIN AND SUMMER STS."

In that letter, now boomeranging back from 1938, Harry had offered himself as a champion of the misunderstood art of dixieland. Being, as he said, "just a novice," he would certainly need to share the byline with some other writer. Then he listed his various requests, and made various guarantees.

I'm going to publish this book, even if it takes a few years.

Harry Brass was born January 16, 1919 in Buffalo.

Harry's mother had Scotch, English, and German origins. His father's father had been born in 1839 in Speyer, Germany, and brought his family to the United States in 1848. In 1861 he enlisted in the Union Army, was wounded at the Second Battle of Bull Run, and was taken prisoner. In 1882 he founded a carriage manufacturing firm, and by the beginning of the century had become a well-known automobile maker.

At 15, Harry, as enterprising as his grandfather, took out a license on a short-wave radio station, W2PYD.

Contacting LaRocca was his first thought upon leaving the Army in 1945, along with applying to the University at Buffalo.

*He kept everything very close to the chest, even with devotees like me.
Sometimes he didn't even respond to my letters.*

CHAPTER THREE

Nick (1891-1905)

When Nick was 15, his father died. They had been tight-knit, the LaRoccas. Often, in the evening, the boy had sat by his father's side, to watch him mend or make new shoes.

He would tell him about the bersaglieri, how they sometimes used a bugle with a valve. Excellent soldiers, the bersaglieri. He would tease his brother about it, who had served in the lowly infantry.

Girolamo LaRocca had left Italy in 1876, aged 22. He'd already held the rank of corporal bugler in the army of Victor Emmanuel II, a bersagliere under the illustrious General La Marmora. He was truly energetic: into his 50s he would compete with the other Italians at vaulting barrels of flour.

Sometimes, on Sundays in those final years of the century, he and some other old veterans of the King of Italy's army would put on little revues at New Orleans' Spanish Fort. People brought their families to watch. Girolamo played the cornet and the guitar.

The old bersaglieri of New Orleans had a mutual aid society, too, to help the Italians of the neighborhood with doctor's bills and the like. They even had their own chapel built at Metairie Cemetery. Girolamo himself took a special interest in Sicilian immigrants, especially anyone from Salaparuta, the town of his birth, from which he was one of the first men to emigrate to New Orleans. He'd help them find houses and jobs.

Salaparuta was a thousand years old. The Arabs had founded it, on an acre of country called Salah in the hills behind the city of Trapani. There, Girolamo had played in the town band, created in 1858 by a priest named Isidoro Oliveri. Don Oliveri even wrote songs for his little orchestra, including one especially for the maestro Mazzarelli, its conductor:

Rejoice, Aphrodite
Rejoice me, my Cupids
And you, my Apollo,
Your choruses chaste.
You Graces and Muses
Rejoice.

Here on this miserable
Dolorous soil
In this land of sorrow
The country of woe,
A note will sound out to
Console.

The chords and the harmonies
That our Mazzarelli plays
Wake the angelic new
Pleasures of art
Among the Sicilians, born to
Despair.

Now greet me my strenuous
Youths, every one of them;
See them well formed in
The musical arts:
The Olympian auspice, a gift
Divine.

Now Girolamo's shoe repair shop stood at 2002 Magazine Street, in New Orleans' Irish Channel.

Dominic James LaRocca, called Nick, fourth child of five, was born April 11, 1889, to Girolamo LaRocca and Vita Denina.

On Sunday afternoons, Girolamo liked to take his children on long walks along the Mississippi, where music would echo faintly from the moored riverboats, which often had their own little orchestras. Sometimes, if they could, they would all come aboard to listen. But other times the bands would come down, and play right there on the wharf.

All of Nick's siblings played music, at least as children: the oldest played the violin, one sister the mandolin and guitar, another the jaw harp. But Nick wouldn't be a musician. He would be a doctor—Girolamo was firm on this point. One of his brothers took cornet lessons instead.

Music, after all, didn't pay. What was a musician? A wretch, Girolamo would say, a tramp. Even he had eventually decided never to play except at home, for the pleasure of his own family, usually something from his military repertoire: "I Bersaglieri Passano" or similar marches. He would play them on the same cornet he'd brought from Sicily.

Nick would risk everything to practice with that old horn, even stealing away to an abandoned house on Jackson Avenue to play in secret. Finally, he reached the point at which ready to show his father what he'd managed to learn on his own. He told Girolamo everything, about how he'd slip off with his horn, and he played what he could for him.

I want you to be a doctor, not a bum.

Girolamo LaRocca wrote something to that effect on paper and fixed it to the wall by the front door of the house, after smashing his old Sicilian cornet with an ax.

The neighbors seemed to concur. They had previously thrown tomatoes, pailfuls of water, garbage and the occasional rock at the aspiring musician.

But Nick worked over his summer vacations, and with the money he saved he bought a used cornet. He found he could stifle its sound by playing in an empty cistern, or inside a concrete depot, whose walls would ring with the improvised runs of his songs.

Sometimes he'd even march down Magazine Street, at the head of a little parade of youths armed with wild, improbable instruments—trash can lids, wooden spoons, cigar boxes—blasting away at his cornet. Then he'd wave an American flag. "Remember the Maine," he'd shout, "to hell with Spain!"

He kept his cornet at the St. Alphonsus parish school. One night, however, he forgot himself, and brought it home without thinking. His father smashed this second cornet to pieces like the first one, and nailed its carcass to the wall in his shop.

Nick got a third cornet, this one almost new, after a couple weeks. This time he took it far away, to the edges of town, to explore its possibilities.

When his father died, Nick left the University School to find work. At the Old French Opera he made a dollar a night as an usher, and began to learn about the world of opera. The money was good: he could finally buy a brand new cornet, which he could finally play at home. He also got his hands on a phonograph, on which he listened to the brass band of John Philip Sousa, the March King.

CHAPTER FOUR

Harry (1946)

It was summer of 1946. Harry had just left the Army, and was taking up his artistic education again.

He'd learned the war was over in quite an unusual way: directly from General Eisenhower. The message had arrived from the Supreme Headquarters Allied Expeditionary Force at 4:10am on May 7, 1945. Brass was stationed in Bad Godesberg, on the Rhine: they'd put him to work at the Advanced Section Communications Zone.

> *07040B May 45*
> *GR 239 URGENT*
> *from SHAEF REF. NO. FWD 20801*
> *SGD. EISENHOWER cite SH CGZ*
> *to ASGZ*
>
> *A representative of the German High Command has signed the unconditional surrender of all German forces on land, air and sea in Europe to the Allied Forces, and to the Soviet High Command at 0141 hours Central European time. All Allied forces are to cease operations at 0001 hours on May 9.*
> *Effective immediately, all Allied offensive operations are to cease. All troops are to remain in their present positions. All movements involved in occupation are to continue. There may be delays in communication as similar orders reach enemy troops. All purely defensive precautions must be taken.*
> *No statement is to be made to the press before the announcement by the three heads of government.*
>
> *SGD. EISENHOWER*

The letter caught Harry by surprise as he was banging out a letter on his old Signal Corps typewriter, a very long letter to his mother.

He yanked his letter out and rolled it up, then got to work. He could scarcely contain his excitement. He transcribed the message into Morse code over the wireless. It was going out to all stations, and, remarkably, not in code.

That summer vacation, for the first time in his life, Harry found himself on his way to the South. He was euphoric. He was going to finally meet the great Dominic James LaRocca.

With hardly any money in his pocket, he boarded a train in Buffalo, changed in Chicago, and was soon steaming toward Louisiana. Three days of travel: he slept in his third-class cars and ate what his mother had packed for him. The round trip ticket had cost $85.

When he got off in New Orleans, he looked around for a cheap hotel, preferably not too far from where the cornetist lived.

My friends, the ones I have left, call me a renaissance man of the 20th Century. It's because I've done so many things. The truth is I was always a dilettante, you know: jack of all trades and master of none, that kind of thing.

After the Original Dixieland Jazz Band had broken up, between the end of 1924 and the beginning of 1925, Nick LaRocca had gone back to New Orleans and taken up the trade he'd learned in youth, construction site carpentry. He would even make himself a pretty little house with an upper story, 928 Jackson Avenue. He drew up the plumbing and electrical plans for it himself. A few black youths of the neighborhood helped him move the materials.

He was a ball of nerves and jet fuel, that powerful little man. He was already divorced from his wife, Vicky, with whom he hadn't had children.

It was to her that he left the little house on Jackson Avenue; he built another on the corner of the same block, 2218 Constance Street. It was smaller than the first house, but had the same structure. He rented out the bottom floor; upstairs was for him and young second wife, Ruth, and one by one their many children.

*

Harry was boiling inside, hotter than the swelter of the New Orleans weather, when he rang the doorbell.

The door opened, and Harry found himself looking at an unfamiliar face. He had not imagined LaRocca so old, so fat and gray and nearsighted. Nick, on the other hand, had the opposite surprise: he hadn't realized his Yankee fan was only a boy of 27, the same age as his own wife, 30 years younger than himself.

I always felt that I wasted my energy on too many things. It's a weakness. I always wished I could dedicate myself to just one thing and do it right. But I could never control my moods. I always ended up getting dragged around from one thing to another.

The old bandleader was kind enough to Harry, but rather than talk he handed off to him a giant stack of photo albums and articles clipped from newspapers; he would have preferred the boy to handle things from there. Then, without a word, he got back to his construction work. He assigned Harry the upstairs veranda as a place to work, with his troop of screaming children for company, and Ruth—a beautiful girl, forever barefoot and solicitous—brought him lemonade.

Harry often wouldn't come in until after dark. Ruth and the kids, waiting for him at the top of the stairs, would clap as he came in.

It was Harry's first attempt to make a book from what he had learned so far, and it was not successful.

CHAPTER FIVE

Nick (1905-1916)

From 1905 to 1916 Nick played in no fewer than ten bands around New Orleans, variously at the Market, on Magazine Street, in Backatown, in the Irish Channel, at the Haymarket café.

I started out with a little group, all strings. They had a set, very sentimental, that they used to play in the houses in the Irish Channel, just playing for cakes and refreshments.

Some of them were "no beer—no music," and played in the evening with the expectation of refreshment in spots along the Gulf Coast: Biloxi, Long Beach, Gulfport, Henderson's Point, Long Town, Pass Christian.

Most of them played ragtime: the guitarist would lead, but eventually every piece would finish in a breakdown, with the leader "calling out" the band members one by one for a solo. Many of these members, including LaRocca, were what they called "fakers"—they couldn't read music and made do with whatever they had, deciphering the chords with their own systems of letters and numbers.

By day, Nick worked. He was a plumber, a carpenter, a demolition man, an electrician, a maintenance man at a print shop. It was, in fact, the printer Tom Gessner who first introduced him to the trombonist Eddie Edwards, at 220 Chartres Street, where LaRocca was spending a break between sets alone on the terrace:

"Nick spends a good part of the day serenading the seagulls with his horn."

Nick and Eddie—Eddie was a "paper man," meaning he could read music—started working together, not only in duets but in electrical installations, during the day around New Orleans. Eddie even got him hired by Braun's Military Band:

"Play harmony but don't play too loud," advised Edwards, "and they'll never know you're a faker." He was right.

In 1914 New Orleans teemed with marching bands: on street corners, on the riverboats, in the city parks. They formed an inevitable part of every event, holidays and funerals and sporting events alike. There were eventually so many bands that band members were in short supply, and the would-be's and novices began swarming into Paul Blum's café at Exchange Place every afternoon.

Nick LaRocca, Eddie Edwards and the clarinetist Alcide Nunez—three fifths of the Original Dixieland Jazz Band—would play with the Reliance Band, too, founded by the celebrated drummer of the city, Jack "Papa" Laine.

Laine ran a lot of bands around the city, many of them less than well-crewed. LaRocca occasionally found himself responsible for running bands of "dummies," literally mannequins in uniform, clutching real instruments, upright as if alive. Atop a horse-drawn wagon, with trumpet, trombone, clarinet and kettledrum, the dummies advertised for shops and events. Up among them sat Nick LaRocca, Leonce Mello, Alcide Nunez, Papa Laine. The crowds ran after them as they cried out what they were selling.

On December 13, 1915, an elegant young nightclub impresario from Chicago, one Harry H. James, was stopped in his tracks at the corner of Canal Street and Royal by the deafening roar of one of Nick's "ballyhoos," the wagon festooned with posters for a featherweight fight between Eddie Coulon and the hometown hero, Pete Herman.

The band was set to earn $7.25 that night.

Back then the trombone and clarinet still played in unison with the cornet. Polyphonic playing, the dixieland style, that was a long way off. But still, there was something innovative in the way those boys were playing ragtime . . .

The following February, after some quick discussions, the street musicians received a telegram from Mr. James, inviting them to Chicago. They left in March, by train, bound for the Windy City:

Schiller's Café on the South Side, then Casino Gardens, where they played for five months.

The drummer Johnny Stein had received the telegram, and ran to LaRocca. They considered whom to bring: Eddie Edwards, on trombone; Alcide "Yellow" Nunez on clarinet; Henry Ragas on keys. They'd go by the name "Stein's Band from Dixie."

Those five boys had never been to the North and had no idea what kind of cold they were in for. Their teeth were chattering. I jumped into the first second-hand clothes store I saw and grabbed some overcoats for them, black. I watched them come out of that shop one by one and I started laughing. They had never seen overcoats before. They looked just like five undertakers.

At Schiller's, some of the regulars, in an access of enthusiasm or simply drunk, would sometimes call out, "Jass it up, boys!" Soon the group was billing itself as "Stein's Dixie Jass Band."

Nick LaRocca explained everything in clear, simple terms. The clarinetist was to play counterpunctually, against the melody. The trombone now had a double job, giving rhythmic and harmonic support. The drums and piano were there to provide a base rhythm.

Nick ran the band like a team of horses, with fierce energy. Even the sound of his cornet had body, had substance.

The dialogues and disputes between the instruments, their laughter, their shrill fights—Nick seemed to have transformed the band into his memories of the French Opera, with its duels and duets, its cavatine and fauxbourdon and potpourri. Fire and amusement, violence and fun: this was LaRocca's key. The "whinny," for example, had been an accidental discovery a few years before: one of his keys had gotten stuck, and in trying to shake it loose he ended up playing something like a horse's whine. Later, Nick tried to use the whinny to achieve a "blue number." Just at the right moment, he would nod to the clarinetist to blow a rooster's cry, and to the trombonist to imitate a jackass' bray; and so came the "breaks" of "Livery Stable Blues," born from the chords of Stephen Adams' "The Holy City."

He was almost obsessed in those days with the sounds of animals. He categorized each motif that came to him in a kind of mental bestiary. "Sensation Rag," "Ostrich Walk," "Tiger Rag" . . .

The tiger's roar, rasped out by the trombone, finally pierced the veil of their obscurity.

One Saturday night some time after 2 o'clock, late in April 1916, a crowd of upright and assiduous ladies of the Anti-Saloon League and the Federal Council of Churches marched into Schiller's on a raid, to expose that den of sin to the *Chicago Herald*:

It was impossible for anyone to be heard. The shriek of women's drunken laughter rivaled the blatant scream of the imported New Orleans Jass Band, which never seemed to stop playing. Men and women sat, arms about each other, singing, shouting, making the night hideous, while their unfortunate brethren and sisters fought in vain to join them.

Stein's band was making just barely $25 per week. They could do better, as LaRocca and Edwards convinced Nunez and Ragas. Stein, however, refused to break his contractual obligations. The discussion that followed grew heated, and Edwards threw a punch at Stein's jaw.

On May 26, 1916, the four rebels, with their curious accents and their miserable suits, quit Schiller's for good. They picked up a new drummer, Anthony Sbarbaro, and a new band was born: the ODJB.

The press took notice of them on July 6, at the Casino Gardens.

The Jass Band hit it off like a whirlwind in next place. The Jass band was a hit from the start and offered the wildest kind of music ever heard outside of a Commanche massacre. There are five men in this band, and they make enough noise to satisfy even a north side bunch out for entertainment . . .

Nunez, during these days, became ever more temperamental and harder to contain. He would skip practice; he would show up to gigs already drunk, or drink up his end of the fee within the night. LaRocca gave him the sack on October 31, 1916 and installed Larry

Shields in his place.

The fiery cornetist had problems of his own, though. He found himself in need of the protection of certain underworld figures of the neighborhood. He acquired a revolver, too. The lovely, athletic blonde he'd been cozying up to, Jesse, turned out to be the boss Joe Bova's girl.

His bandmates quickly dubbed him Nick the Gunman.

All the talk about the band caught the attention of a theater agent named Max Hart, who proposed a regular show at Reinsenweber's Café, in New York, for $750 a week.

CHAPTER SIX

Harry (1947-1957)

For 20 years, Harry Brass devoted himself to writing—in one way or another. He had taken a degree in architecture from Buffalo's Albright Art School in 1949, and immediately began work writing electrical aerospace manuals, first for Bell in Buffalo, then for Boeing in Seattle, and finally for Boeing's Minuteman missile project.

He also dabbled in graphic design and animation, painted landscapes, wrote radio plays and played the trombone in his spare time, for his own amusement.

I am an individualist and I'm anti-social. A natural loner. My personal philosophers are Epicurus and Thoreau. Maybe I stopped thinking about these kinds of questions too young—questions about myself, I mean, about who I am.

In his new Jaguar, Harry Brass left Buffalo and crossed Pennsylvania, Virginia, Tennessee, Alabama, Mississippi, thousands of miles of highway punctuated with a few nights in motels, to reach New Orleans on May 4, 1957.

An unseasonable chill hung all along the Gulf coast, starting in Biloxi. Miles and miles would run by without another car on the road. But the highway that ran along the sea seemed to be suspended permanently in a lovely bright morning. Brass was motoring along at 45 miles per hour, well above his normal speed on a trip this long: after 11 years, he was going back to see Nick LaRocca, completely by surprise and to determine the fate of this book that he'd worked on ceaselessly, if inconsistently and incoherently.

His last night on the road he spent at the Southwinds Motor Court. There, after certain calculations of average speed and distance and the price of motels he knew he could scarcely afford, he slept, woke, shaved with care and put on his suit of white linen.

Would the difficult, untalkative LaRocca ever open that cantankerous heart of his?

Once on Canal Street, Brass consulted a telephone listing at a municipal building. The address hadn't changed: *LaRocca, Domenic J. (carp.), 2216-18 Constance Street.* The girl at reception gave him directions.

It was about noon when he parked his car just outside the house of the cornetist. From the sidewalk, he could see the old man's children romping about on the upstairs veranda. Then he walked up to the door, like a man steeling himself for the firing squad; extended a finger; rang the bell. The door opened. There, unshod, stood Nick LaRocca. Eleven years had passed since they'd last looked at each other; the old bandleader didn't seem to have changed very much. Brass, on the other hand, now looked the part of the gentleman, well- turned-out and self-assured, at least in comparison to how he'd seemed. He reintroduced himself. LaRocca remembered him and the first, failed attempt at a biography. He asked him into the ground floor, which the LaRocca's now occupied as well, and Brass asked him to oblige him with just a quarter hour of conversation, no more, and not necessarily now but when he wanted.

LaRocca responded that, now that he was retired, he could talk for a week straight if Brass wanted.

In that moment, the biographer could feel his life twisting sharply off its track and into something new. He was not going to let the old jazzman's sudden tractability go to waste.

That same morning, after loading up Brass with old photocopies, LaRocca took him to see the old, dying Harry James, the same that had first engaged him in Chicago in 1915 and thus brought jazz to the North. Then he took him to the bar of his cousin, Victor LaRocca, and stood him a drink.

Nick was enthusiastic about the book.

For his own part, Brass' mind raced through the possibilities, not only of *writing* the book, but of creating his own publishing house ad hoc, and taking care of his own printing and distribution and promotion... In the meantime, however, Brass had to go back to work: he was soon to be transferred to Eglin Air Force Base, in Florida.

That evening, as he sat at the Monkey Bar with his gin and tonic, a dark, lovely girl approached him, perching neatly on the barstool just next to his.

Briefly, in 1950, I was engaged. It was about the closest I've ever come to that hell called marriage. All the same, I don't know how many miserable hours of my life I've spent in nightclubs, running after girls, spending a fortune . . .

Brass, at the summit of an emotion that made him reel like a drunk, decided to suspend his contract with Bell Aircraft, for whom he'd been writing installation manuals for aircraft carrier missile launchers. He would work exclusively on the history of Nick LaRocca and his band, and he would take the first flight possible back to the South, to Louisiana, to see his cornetist.

On July 23, 1957, somewhere in the sky around Charleston, Brass fastened his seat belt during a gust of turbulence. The tumult bothered him less than the fact that he had to put his turkey sandwich and iced tea on the floor, although he conceded that the way the wing looked like it wanted to bend off was mildly troubling.

On the ground in New Orleans, he rented a limousine and ordered the man to take him to the Jung Hotel, with its 1,200 rooms and air conditioning and television sets and various other refinements.

The indulgence of those refinements kept him, the next morning, from actually seeing LaRocca. But that afternoon he made it, and the next four days passed in a frenzy of work. Thereafter they took a reasonable pace. The old man dug up a typewriter and gave him all the old letters he could find, as well as cold water in a pitcher as needed.

Brass, after work, would spend his evenings in the nightclubs, listening to music, collecting testimony, and in rather expensive gallantries. He even managed to satisfy his desire for the Jung's sumptuous restaurant, the Charcoal Room: grilled steak and, that marvel, a salad tossed under his eyes. A young black waiter, all in white, took pains to refresh his water with a monstrous blizzard of ice cubes.

Every day began with the usual complaints about the good old days and the general decline of the world. This would lead to an actual conversation, one that grew denser with allusion, richer and more confused as it went on before drying up and returning to fatigue and boredom on the part of the elderly host. Weeks of this passed.

The old man never missed an opportunity, either, to see if he couldn't make his young devotee into a kind of Trojan horse; if only he could cajole something incriminating out of some of these old New Orleans jazzmen, and write it down, LaRocca would be sitting on a handy bit of proof in the event of a future lawsuits. There was no end of the liars, he told Brass, simply no end of the liars who needed unmasking and punishment.

CHAPTER SEVEN

Nick (1917)

The *New York Times*, January 15, 1917, ran this remarkable, nearly full-page ad:

MARGARET HAWKESWORTH'S
"PARADISE"

The Smartest, Most Beautiful and Most Modern Ballroom
in America

In the New Reisenweber Building, at

Eighth Avenue and 58th Street

announces

The First Sensational Amusement Novelty of 1917

"THE JASZ BAND"

Direct from its amazing success in Chicago, where it has
given modern dancing new life and a new thrill. The Jasz
Band is the latest craze that is sweeping the nation like a
musical thunderstorm.

"THE JASZ BAND"

Comes exclusively, to "Paradise" First of all New
York Ballrooms, and will open for a run TONIGHT
(Monday). You've Just Got to Dance When You Hear It.

No one knew what this strange music could be. Indeed, for some time no one tried to dance. Some people protested and hissed the band. Someone shouted out, "Kick them out!" The manager of the club had to actually be told that this music was meant to be danced to. Finally, two or three brave couples pressed forward. Immediately the crowd poured in after them, curious to try these new steps, these mad rhythms. The madness was voluptuous. It was contagious. New York awoke the next morning to find itself conquered by jazz.

In the following days, the New York police had to post patrolmen on horseback at the entrance of Reisenweber's to regulate the coming and going of the hordes of dancers. What this new band brought with them was something altogether new. Gone was the rigid ragtime hop; in was a new frenzy.

The boys from Louisiana had armored themselves in tuxedos, but this didn't stop LaRocca and Edwards from running upstairs one evening to fix an electrical outage at the 400 Club Room, which had caused the lights to cut out on them as they played.

The powerful shock waves of Tony Sbarbaro's big parade drums shook the walls; Edwards' trombone blasted and slurred with brassy bass notes that rattled every champagne glass in the room; the strident screams of Shields' clarinet echoed down the mirrored corridors and made people in the street stop to look about.

The band's pay went from $750 a week to $1,000.

On February 2, 1917, the *New York Times* decided on "jazz" as the standard spelling of the new music, having tried and discarded others: "jass," "jasz," "jaz." Shortly thereafter, to distinguish themselves from a legion of imitators, the group changed its own name to the Original Dixieland Band—"Creators of Jazz."

"Oh, boy!" the crowd shouted on the dancefloor. The draw was impossible to resist. Some of them collapsed with exhaustion, unable to keep dancing.

In January 1917, the boys recorded two tracks with Columbia, "Darktown Strutters' Ball" and "Back Home in Indiana." The thunderous band got its own separate recording room, usually reserved for opera singers and string quartets. Ragtime and jazz had never been heard there. The session was disastrous, though. There were even workmen hammering in the studio while they played, which made it into the record.

The double was released a few months later, but only because Victor had picked the band up a few weeks after their humiliation at Columbia. Immediately, a 78 appeared on the market: "Livery Stable Blues" and "Dixieland Jass Band One-Step," which Victor marketed aggressively. It was February 26, 1917, and the record was number 18255 in the Victor Talking Machine Company catalogue. An announcement ran in the *Victor Record Review* on March 7:

We can't tell you what a "Jass" Band is because we don't know ourselves. As for what it does—*it makes dancers want to dance more—and more—and yet more! . . . You'll want to hear the first Victor Record by this organized disorganization—it's a "winner." "Livery Stable Blues," a fox trot, and "Dixieland Jass Band One-Step" are playing with charming ferocity and penetration.*

"Livery Stable Blues" alone sold over a million copies. LaRocca would always hold it to be a kind of personal alchemy, a fantasia on the notes of a hymn called "The Holy City." But it became better known for Shields' cock-a-doodle-doo, Edwards' braying and LaRocca's horse whinny, with his third valve barely pressed.

All this time, in the band's home, people were beginning to worry. New Orleans' *Times-Picayune* took pains to disassociate itself from that "indecent story syncopated and counterpointed," that "musical vice." "Livery Stable Blues" also landed LaRocca in court, the first of a lifelong series of lawsuits. Central to most of them was the question of copyright: there was never a shortage of self-proclaimed writers and composers for any given song, each contesting the title. A few of them would rush to trademark a piece and the others would drag them to court. Not even the best-disposed and most patient judges could ever really resolve this ongoing melee: slight manipulations of wording or chords, outright lies, plagiarism, accusations without proof, blackmail, naked spite, musical ignorance, contradictions, ingenuity, bad faith, innocent errors of transcription. It was impossible to unravel it all.

There were several people in the Schiller's Café and one girl in particular was evidently feeling jolly and sky-larking to the amusement of the boys in the band, which prompted LaRocca to pick up the cornet and play a horse whine on it. Everybody laughed within hearing distance of it, and I told him at the time it would be a good stunt to put this horse whine in a number, and he said he had it in a number. I, of course, asked him what number it was, and he replied, "a blue number." I told him some time we might try it and it might prove a good number to us.

I heard all this from the pavilion, and later I told him to add that sound to a blues number. It would really shake people up. He tried it out the next day: that bitter, liquid clarinet of Yellow Nunez squawked, and then it clucked; Nick did the whinny, and then I responded to them with a big, sad moooo with the trombone.

The "Livery Stable Blues" suit turned out to be Alcide Nunez's revenge on LaRocca for throwing him out, back in the Casino Gardens days. They'd never bothered to copyright the piece properly; so Nunez did. LaRocca republished it in turn as "Barnyard Blues." The whole picaresque ended up before the Northern District Court of Illinois, while the press clamored for more. Intrigues, doubts, unresolved mysteries abounded, and the judge, George A. Carpenter, could only just wriggle out of it unscathed.

After all, who could ever—in that moment more than any—put jazz, its birth and its mysteries, on the witness stand?

Nick LaRocca, whom the *Chicago American* was now calling the "Jazz Kid," sat in the front row of the gallery on October 11, 1917, displaying his patent leather boots, his apple-green sport coat, and his bright striped shirt.

Chicago's *Daily News* ran a headline that morning about the "Discoverer of Jazz" "elucidating" his invention to the court. It referred to LaRocca wryly as "the Jazz Kid himself, the giddy boy whose brain first got the big idea . . . He identified himself as the genuine Columbus of the Jazz, the Sir Isaac Newton of the latest dance craze."

In his New Orleans drawl, he explained how the idea of the animal noises first came to him; and, unabashedly, he did not hesitate to declare himself the linchpin of the blues *tout court*, beyond "Livery Stable Blues."

"Might I ask what exactly the blues *are?*" asked the judge.

"The blues is jazz. The jazz is blues. The blues means to the jazz what the rag means to ragtime, see?"

Nunez's testimony was rather more compelling. He maintained that he was one of several coathors of the song in question.

The court heard the testimony of various experts regarding the songs of birds and the sounds of horses. The judge himself nearly surrendered to temptation, and asked for the song to be played for the edification of the court; but he thought better of it.

On October 12, 1917, Judge Carpenter decided:

> *The finding of the Court is therefore that neither Mr. LaRocca and his associates nor Mr. Nunez and his associates conceived the idea of this melody . . . I venture to say that no living human being could listen to that result on the phonograph and discover anything musical in it, although there is a wonderful rhythm, something which will carry you along especially if you are young and a dancer.*
>
> *The finding of the Court will be that neither the plaintiff nor the defendant is entitled to a copyright.*

The cornetist and his dixielanders catapulted themselves, blindly, into performances of this hit that no longer quite belonged to them. LaRocca would never say more than "Let's go with this one;" he'd play a few beats of whatever happened to be swirling around in his head, then he'd set the tempo. Then every man played his own part, scarcely paying attention to the chords and refrains of the whole ensemble, each waiting tensley for the savage general harmony.

When Henry Ragas died and a vacancy opened at the keys, Nick LaRocca would later declare, "I don't know how many pianists we tried out before we found one who didn't read music!" Redoing the written scores, he feared, would dampen all the energy that the band had been trying to harness.

When the United States declared war on Germany in April 1917, the entire entertainment industry needed that kind of energy, that electric jolt on the staff line.

It might have been true that LaRocca and Larry Shields were the principal authors of "Livery Stables Blues," but often the whole group assumed its authorship together. The ODJB's payments were distributed equally as well, at least for a while, with LaRocca as leader and Eddie Edwards—held even by his friends to be lazy and a bit of a snob—as administrator. Nevertheless, he was the only man in the band who could read music, although he hid this from the public as a matter of professional reputation.

By the end of 1917, though, LaRocca had assumed all administrative responsibilities, including the signing of contracts. For his sharpness as an impresario, Edwards rebaptized him "Joe Blade."

"Joe Blade," in the meantime—attributed author of "Tiger Rag," "Sensation Rag," "Ostrich Walk," "Skeleton Jungle," "Clarinet Marmalade," "Fidgety Feet" and others—was falling more and more into a state of confusion on the stage, during shows.

With so many musical ideas straining to break loose from the brain in which they were imprisoned, a certain amount of confusion was inevitable. Certain pet phrases of LaRocca's, common to several of his compositions, proved to be perilous traps for himself and the band during performances. He would sometimes start out playing one number and end up playing another, much to the consternation of his fellow musicians. Dancers close enough to the bandstand might see Edwards drop his horn and shout to LaRocca, "Hey, Joe! Where you goin'?"

CHAPTER EIGHT

Harry (1958-1959)

Brass decided to take up the trombone again, seriously this time, some 20 years after his adolescent infatuation with it. Within six months he'd mastered it.

He shelved his missile manual writing and, joining the New Charleston Chasers, played every evening for five years at a restaurant called the Speakeasy, near Niagara Falls. Sometimes the group played elsewhere, in parades or at picnics or family parties. But Brass' main business continued to be the story of the five boys from New Orleans.

In February 1959, he made plans to return down South, where he would hopefully work with LaRocca on the story's final chapters, and with an editor to establish the graphic and promotional details of the published book. It was his fourth visit to old Nick and perhaps his most memorable. The long drive down, and the 15 days he spent in New Orleans (February 22 to March 9, 1959) were not without surprises for the would-be biographer.

Having covered almost a thousand miles, Harry left his motel room in Memphis under a torrent of rain. No one was out on the roads. Driving somewhere between 70 and 90 miles an hour, Brass covered about 200 miles in less than three hours. He enjoyed it. He said to himself on the journey down that if, for traffic or bad weather, he had to slow down to 20 miles per hour, he'd do it without complaint. He also noted that black motorists were more scrupulous, more respectful of the rules than he was: he wondered if that wasn't their understanding that their penalties for infractions were much heavier than his own would be.

Around 11 he pulled into a diner called Early Gary's for a breakfast heavy enough to make him skip lunch. At 4 o'clock, some 75 miles from his destination, he smashed into a car coming down from the Mississippi hills, a yellow Plymouth with three children aboard. He'd slammed the brakes just as the car appeared in a tiny intersection, but it was too late. He spun out into a fallow field. No one was injured; just scratched up or stunned.

A young black man, of very dark complexion, scrambled over to Brass, who hadn't brought himself to get out of the car yet. "You all right, sir?" he asked. "Shook up a bit?"

Strangely, I was fairly calm, but I felt myself sinking into despair. I was drowning in a kind of depression. The more I thought about it, the more inclined I was to believe that there was a touch of extrasensory perception about that accident. As soon as that car appeared I knew the driver wasn't going to stop, and I got all clammy. Maybe I caused the whole thing, by suggestion or by "interference" in the driver's brain—who knows. Maybe if I had been thinking something else he would have been able to brake in time.

The police would eventually confirm that the other driver was at fault. Brass had his car towed to Baton Rouge; he tipped the driver for taking him and his suitcase along.

They were astonished to meet a writer in the flesh. Well, they got used to the idea by the time we got to Baton Rouge.

At the hotel, the two young men from the tow truck helped Harry with his trunks full of suits, his sacks of tinned food, his stationary, roadmaps, piles of books, his files and attaché cases, his trombone, his typewriter . . .

Brass quickly realized his clothes were too heavy for the Southern climate. He was sweating. He called his mother, telling her all about his road accident; his brother Jim noted that he might be able to write the damages off on his taxes. Then he went downstairs to sip a vanilla ice cream float, and returned to take refuge in uneasy sleep.

The next day at 9 o'clock sharp he was seated in the waiting room of his editor, Don Feelgood of the Louisiana State University Press. Feelgood phoned around to find him a room on campus, then loaned him his own miserable old Plymouth. Brass hired a porter to load up all his belongings into that jalopy, which he guessed to be worth no more than $20, dented and run down and short of breath.

It wasn't like Don was risking a thousand bucks on that car, not in one afternoon.

Harry's sense of direction was abysmal: he wandered the campus for two hours, asking a score of students for directions, before he arrived at his rooms. They were in a tower that dominated the campus.

The room wasn't bad, Harry observed; quite nice, in fact. He had combed through it minutely, sink and toilet, bedframe and walls, the floorplan, the general dimensions, the conditions of the closet and the desk, the quality of the view. Five dollars a night was quite a deal.

He was in the mood for steak and asked someone for recommendations. The campus restaurant, however, was dry. Harry, at the waiter's sly intimation, slipped out between his order and the arrival of his dinner for a double martini at the bar next door. There should have been plenty of time for it, but of course there wasn't: the Tiger Lounge was half a mile away, and Harry, stumbling out, gave a dollar for a ride from a gas station attendant to make it back in time. The martini itself had cost him 80 cents.

It rained the next day. Harry ran down early to Allied Imported Cars to look at his smashed Jaguar.

I started crying. That car was a person to me; I always gave her the best. I felt like a deadbeat father. I couldn't get an apology out, not even a word, I was so upset.

The mechanics didn't bother giving Brass an estimate. He left them and wandered into the showroom, where he saw a Jaguar of the almost same model: an XK-150 roadster, white with a black interior. Harry sat at the wheel and choked down a sob at the thought of his XK-140.

It wasn't the last of Brass' automotive lovers to die in a road accident: he would crash his '66 coupé as well. The true companions of Brass' life were:

A 1953 Jaguar XK-120 Spider;
a 1955 Jaguar XK-140 MC Spider;
a 1962 Jaguar XK-E Spider;
a 1966 Jaguar XK-E coupé;
a 1966 Jaguar XK-E Spider;
a 1968 Lamborghini 400-GT; and
a 1972 Volvo P-1800.

For the moment, however, Harry had things to do. He had to go down to his publisher's, for one thing, and choose illustrations for his book. Don had admired the recently-submitted preface, which raised Harry's spirits some.

In fact, the next three days in Baton Rouge were frenetic. He spent them packing up and shipping his baggage, devouring filet mignon, gulping down martinis, wrapping up unfinished letters, checking and rechecking stock market values, making deposits and withdrawals at various banks, and snapping photos of Don in his office, where the man was busy grappling with the extravagances of his other authors.

On the afternoon of the last day of February 1959, Harry boarded the bus for New Orleans. He had to seal a few final arrangements with the Maestro, as he sometimes called him, relishing the Italian pronunciation.

The first evening in Crescent City had to be spent verifying that nothing had changed since his last visit. Small things had changed, but very small. On Bourbon Street, Harry spent the night with a showgirl from Texas named Margie, whom he'd engaged at the Flamingo Club.

He was staying at the New Hotel Monteleone, on Royal Street.

He spent the next morning first at the Jaguar dealership at 840 Carondelet Street, then on a martini crawl: from the Carousel to the Old Absinthe House and on to the Vieux Carré, Broussard's, Jim Moran's, and finally the Diamond, where he took the risk of drawing a portrait of the barman to pay his bill.

He settled his stomach afterward with a lunch of turtle soup, at which point he required a nap. He woke up startled in mid afternoon. The telephone was ringing: it was Nick. The old cornetist wanted to see him the next day. He agreed and immediately called Phil Zito, an old warhorse of the neighborhood jazz scene, long retired; he talked him into an evening at the Variety Club, promising fried chicken and Doberge cake. After dinner, Bingo: Harry won an electric frying pan and presented it gallantly to Phil. Later he went back to Bourbon Street, where he spent a couple hours listening to a band in the Dream Room. At two he left to meet Pam, barely 18 and the main attraction at the Guys & Dolls Club, 418 Bourbon Street.

She was a specialist, Pam, already a striptease veteran, and she came from Alabama. Harry, on seeing her onstage, reflected on the many Southern finalists in the Miss America contest. His reverie cut short when he saw her approaching his table. He turned to the manager. The magic words at the Guys & Dolls, to have a girl for a night, were *buy out!*, and the floor manager would decide whether to grant the man's wish or not.

At 3 o'clock, after a clumsy hour of something like conversation and a bar tab that made him shudder, Pam took his arm and they went out into the deserted street. She swallowed her smirk and whispered, in the dark, that he was the first client she'd ever left with like this. At a little hotel on Felicity Street they climbed narrow stairs, step by creaking step.

There's a fog of 40 years, more than 40 years, blown in by Mother Memory, that keeps me from remembering that night, the details anyway. I wish I'd written more in my diary, but I was afraid my family might see it. I remember the queen bed, what they used to call a matrimonial bed, and this sensational girl laying on it with her blonde hair everywhere; how nonchalant she was about it, too, and her pubic hair the color of honey she'd trimmed to the shape of her G string.

He woke up with a start at noon. Pam and her lovely body dissolved from his thoughts. He had missed his morning appointment at LaRocca's. He snatched up the telephone. "He just left," said Ruth LaRocca. "He's furious. He waited three hours for you."

Harry ran out onto Canal Street for a taxi, just missing Pam, who was headed the opposite direction.

Soon he was sitting with Nick and his brother, Buddy LaRocca, and one of their friends. The boys had business to discuss with Harry. They had a case against one George Taines for various offenses: would Harry sign his name to a statement for the court?

I didn't like doing him dirty like that. Frankly, I think he's an honest character. But I wasn't ever going to convince Nick of that, and I couldn't afford to turn my back on him and his friends.

The New Orleans Jaguar dealership called in the meantime. They weren't going to consider an exchange, with his car in its condition, certainly not for the terms Brass suggested. It meant going by streetcar, which in the end didn't bother him, they were so old and elegant and vaguely magical.

The next two days he spent at research, either at Tulane or the LaRocca Collection; the nights were reserved for steaks, drinks and strippers. On the third day he went back to LaRocca.

Let me tell you, it took some work to calm him down when he found the error I made in the last chapter. I'd made Shields look more important than him. He'll never forgive me for that. And in any case you can never be sure that he really trusts you. His persecution complex eats at him; it keeps him awake at night.

That night in the French Quarter, at the Court of the Two Sisters, he sipped a mint julep with deliberation, then called for a game hen and shrimp remoulade. Turning up Magazine Street on his way home, he ran into Buddy LaRocca, and the two popped in somewhere for a drink. Brass saw that the LaRocca fire blazed with Nick's presence or without it: some unfortunate at the bar happened to mention the music critic Edmond Pouchon, and it was only Brass' quick intervention that kept Buddy out of a fight.

Two days before the end of his idyll, Brass made one more discovery: breakfast at Brennan's. Why had he waited this long! Two Herbsaint drips, eggs Hussarde, and chicory coffee. The world was warmer and sweeter after a meal like that. Then he made his way, with some misgiving, back to the Monteleone, to rewrite the chapter that had so offended LaRocca. The new text wasn't much better. He called Pam and arranged another night with her.

The waiter at Brennan's welcomed him back that next morning: two more Herbsaint drips, a parmesan omelet, creole cream cheese and a bottle of rosé. He needed fuel: those miserable last few pages weren't going to write themselves. And in fact he dashed them off that very morning at the hotel. LaRocca looked them over and approved.

That night he ate with a professor named Gogan, whom the editor had brought on to help with the final proof. The man, it turned out, knew nothing, practically nothing about jazz.

His questions made my morale sink like a stone. I was actually embarrassed. He wanted to hear gossip, inventions, exaggerations: mortal sins for a historian. He also told me that the subtitle, A True Story of the World's First Jazz Band, *was excessive. He wanted to drop the "true" and the "world's." Maybe the old professor was right, in a way, but I was thinking of the publicity, of the advertising . . .*

CHAPTER NINE

Nick (1918-1921)

At the end of 1917, while the ODJB was making the rounds of Reisenweber's, Keith's Colonial Theater, Sunday concerts and the occasional, wild private party, something unheard of was happening in New Orleans. Storyville, the old red-light district and the ODJB's spiritual home, was closing. The cabarets, the bands, ragtime singers were silent. The whores and orchestras had to go home.

The Department of War had decided to ban major concentrations of prostitution within a five mile radius of a military base. On October 2, the mayor ordered the sporting houses demolished. The final diaspora of the working girls and pimps took place on the night between November 12 and 13.

Nick LaRocca followed the theme with simplicity, with austerity, with sharp sonority, without flourishes or improvisations and without any "growl" at all. He was playing faster than usual, carried by some uncontainable force and yet with a compactness, too. They were fast, these boys; they were doing something with these syncopated dance tunes that other bands simply couldn't.

The first echoes of the war reached the ODJB in May 1918, when they played on a parade float down Broadway as part of a war bonds drive. But then the draft summons came, first for LaRocca and then for his bandmates.

The cornetist went, as summoned, to a recruiting office in New York. He'd long had a tic, a spasm in his left shoulder, he said; he could demonstrate it to the unsympathetic Army doctors present. They left him off, but for weeks federal agents followed him in the street or otherwise kept an eye on him.

Shields, the clarinetist, got off on account of his nerves. Sbarbaro the drummer was still too young to be drafted. But Eddie Edwards was sent out, July 30, 1918, to join the 152nd Depot Brigade of the Rainbow Division. A new trombonist, Emile "Bootmouth" Christian, filled in for him.

Ragas' health, in the meantime, was deteriorating, eaten away by alcohol. The Spanish flu that fall would finish the devastation: he died at Bellevue Hospital, February 18, 1919, aged 28. Joseph Russel Robinson, soon to be author of hits like "Margie" and "Palesteena," would take the unfortunate Ragas' place.

When the Armistice of November 11, 1918 ended the war, the Jazz Age had definitively reached Europe. The ODJB signed a ten week contract with a London impresario. It promised over $1,000 per week for concerts at the Hippodrome.

On March 25, 1918, the Original Dixieland Jazz Band recorded "Tiger Rag" for the first time, a track destined for immortality. LaRocca claimed authorship for this hit, which African American bands in New Orleans had been playing for years under the simple title "Number 2." This is but one example of his arrogance, his refusal to acknowledge the black and creole contributions to jazz.

They set sail from New York Harbor March 22, 1919, with Mrs. Shields and Mrs. Robinson in tow. They landed in Liverpool on the first of April, and by evening their train had reached London. The played the Hippodrome for the first time on the 7th, to clamorous applause: a number of American soldiers were still stationed there, and had come out to see their compatriots.

On April 12 they debuted at the Palladium. The London press was not stingy with their criticism; the general drift was that this music was a weed in their musical garden, and needed uprooting in a hurry. But concerts in Glasgow followed, and soon England's Columbia had them in the studio for a new disk. They wanted nice, melodic dance numbers.

I don't really know why they wanted to deny that I wrote "Tiger Rag."

I did basically write it. Sure, I used some ideas that had been floating around or years, ones I used to hear as a kid. "Tiger Rag" starts like a tango, except I padded it with a few extra notes. Then comes the second part, which is just "London Bridge is Falling Down" in stop time. The next strain is based on the harmonies from "National Emblem March," which I think is one of Sousa's. You know: "Oh, the monkey wrapped his tail around the flagpole. You saw his asshole." That one. The last bit comes from the oom-pah stuff that the German bands used to play in New Orleans.

The end of the war had brought a new desire to live life and enjoy it. Even the royal family came out to the Savoy in Westminster on June 28, 1919 to celebrate the Treaty of Versailles, accompanied by generals and dignitaries, all of whom danced. Marshals Foch and Pétain were there, as was General Pershing.

The Marine Corps Band was commissioned for the ceremony, but the ODJB played for the party. The guests stared, bewildered. Some of them shouted: "Go on! That's it! That's it!" When "Tiger Rag" rang out in the Savoy ballroom, a wave of mess uniforms and glittering jewels swept over the dancefloor.

The schedule book of the band's 17-month stay in England shows that they played privately for the Prince of Wales—a "command performance," as it were. Lord Donegall, at whose suggestion it was held, seems to have joined them on drums.

> *Dear Mr. Brass,*
>
> *On page 129 of the book you write about a "command performance." I believe I told you not to use that story . . . I can't tell how angry I am about this after all the trouble I've taken on in my life just for trying to tell the truth. Now with this statement you're making ME a <u>LIAR</u>. I'm very embarrassed about this. I'm sure I have a CC of the letter I sent you where I told you we only played at the Savoy Hotel, with all the crowned heads of Europe and Persia etc. there. I told you that this was not material for the book.*
>
> *Also the title* The Story of the Dixieland Band *is a mistake. We were only ever called the Original Dixieland*

Jazz Band. Mr. Brass I think you should think less about women and more about your work!

It was the third of April, 1960; the book would launch on the 17th. It was too late, in other words, for corrections. Brass wrote his idol back in a rush. No, it wasn't Russel Robinson who gave him this information. (Just the possibility that Brass might be in contact with the other bandmates was enough to throw LaRocca into a lather of jealous rage.) LaRocca himself had told him so, during Brass' first visit in 1946; the details in question were already present in the 1947 manuscript, which LaRocca had read and approved. The 1957 manuscript had the same details, and that had survived the cornetist's scrutiny as well. By now it might be best not to make a fuss and risk upsetting the editor.

My editor might start asking questions about the rest of the book, you see. I had promised him that it was completely accurate. In fact I have to admit that I lightly fictionalized a few details here and there. I had to, if I wanted to see this book on the bookstore shelves. If you didn't mean so much to me, Mr. LaRocca, I would have given up on this project decades ago, given up discouraged. Even if you hated me I'd still keep up my battle to see the most important man in the history of American music recognized. Maybe I'm not a great historian, but the greatest honor of my life and my greatest source of pride is that you entrusted the story of the ODJB to me.

The ODJB was back at Rectors' on June 29, 1919, then at the Palais de Danse in Hammersmith. Robinson didn't like these new engagements and quit the band. Billy Jones, an English pianist, succeeded him.

Interviewed by the *Palais Dancing News* in April 1920, LaRocca declared that, "Jazz is the assassination, the murdering, the slaying of syncopation. I would even go so far as to confess that we are musical anarchists."

The band left England at 8:40pm, July 8, 1920, aboard the SS *Finland*. They landed in New York ten days later. LaRocca had reasons for quitting England that had nothing to do with music or business: he'd had a number of indiscreet adventures in London, and the consequences were beginning to worry him. It's even said that a certain Lord Harrington, whose teenage daughter had shared LaRocca's apartment and then born his child, stomped up and down the docks at Southampton with a pistol, looking for the cornetist. That LaRocca had played the cad seemed, even to his friends, rather difficult to refute.

In fact, in the last few weeks of his London residency, LaRocca's wife Vicky (from whom he'd soon be divorced) arrived unannounced from New Orleans, where tales of her husband's trespasses had reached her. She finally caught up with him on Pall Mall, where he was out on a Sunday stroll with the girl who considered herself his fiancée, pushing their baby in a pram.

Back in New York, Edwards (who had left) and Robinson both joined the band.

Joe, take a tip from me, from what I understand Old Man Harrington is going to fill you full of bullets if you ever put your foot in England again. So be careful and watch yourself if you ever intend to come back to England.

On September 25, 1920, the ODJB debuted at the Ziegfeld Follies on Broadway, where LaRocca met an electric, fast-talking Polish girl named Gilda Gray. Gray was about to make a fast new version of the foxtrot, called the shimmy, popular all over the country. It was the emblem of a new moral rebellion.

Nick LaRocca, whose talent as a dancer rivaled his genius as a musician, would often jump down from the stage to dance with crowd, or "shaking his busted shoulder," as he called his personal version of the shimmy. Variety noted with astonishment that, in concerts, "one of the players shimmies while playing."

Russel Robinson's clamorous creativity carried them again and again to the RCA Victor studios for new recordings. The first of these was the single "Margie." But the band had to uphold their end of a new bargain. These new records were to be "sweet jazz"—not the wild, uninhibited music of their early career. To enforce the terms of the new bargain, the Victor studio heads enlisted a tenor saxophonist to play with them. The saxophone clashed hideously with the trumpet, for which LaRocca had agreed to substitute his cornet. But business was business. The saxophonist's name was Benny Krueger.

Other musicians joined Krueger and the ODJB in those years: Frank Signorelli and Henry Vanicelli on the piano, Don Parker on sax, Artie Seaberg on clarinet.

On December 30, 1920, while the band was cutting "Sweet Mamma" at the Victor studios, LaRocca (who was standing next to the collecting horn) put down his trumpet and sang out, "Yes *suh*! Sweet mamma, papa's getting mad!" It is the only known recording of his voice, excluding the *March of Time* episode of 1936. But it was the sort of thing LaRocca had taken to calling out in shows, to draw an effect from the audience: "Yes *suh!* That's the tiger!" he would shout in "Tiger Rag."

Briefly, the group engaged a minstrel show singer, Al Bernard. But this was short-lived.

On the first of December 1920 they cut "Bow Wow Blues;" they would wait 15 years before they worked with Victor again. This track featured the falsetto of a poodle and a bloodhound's howl. Animal sounds were hardly new material for the band; they were very nearly their stock in trade. Indeed, on April 20, 1921, several animal behaviorists and other professors invited the boys into the Central Park Zoo in New York, to the mystification of the other visitors, to play for the animals; they hoped to study the beasts' reaction. The hyenas seemed to respond to the sound of the clarinet; the orangutan preferred the cornet, and the lions roared back at the trombone. Other animals were put to the test, but the newspapers proclaimed the star of the experiment to be the polar bear, who alone got up and danced.

The press photographers couldn't get enough of LaRocca playing with his trumpet between the bars of the bear's cage, inches from its nose, or into the trunk of an elephant, held up by a keeper's hand.

The recordings were consistently good until July 17, 1918. Even afterwards, they kept a certain aggression and compactness, as well as the novelty effects. LaRocca, of course, vigorously maintained that everything the ODJB did was basically improvised. It's one more of his unfounded claims: in fact the band arranged and practiced their songs exactly, without variation between performances, for years and years. Nevertheless, by 1921 the limits of their style had emerged. They started playing everything forte, without subtlety; the clockwork of their performance, down to where they took their breaths, had become rigid and repetitive.

On June 15, 1921, the ODJB signed a 12 week contract at Café La Marne in Atlantic City, where they alternated sets with a curious singer named Sophie Jucker, who would challenge the boys to nail-biting games of poker.

In November 1921 they toured Pennsylvania. When they wrapped up, Larry Shields, who had invented the "noodling" style for the clarinet, announced his retirement. The band went to New York, where they played the Balconades Ballroom with a lineup that changed continuously. That engagement lasted until mid-March 1922, when LaRocca contracted pneumonia.

Exactly two months later, LaRocca spent a night in the drunk tank, with about 15 other men and ten girls—all of them involved in the theater or music scene—on account of a too-well-refreshed private party that got out of hand. The police showed up at about 3 o'clock at West 49th Street, number 11; the charge, crowed the morning news, was "immoral conduct."

That year, 1921, was the year that jazz was outlawed—more or less.

CHAPTER TEN

Harry (1959-1960)

Nick recommended that his biographer debunk a number of lies and calumnies about himself and the band that had their origins in "Mouse-Face Spargo"—that is, in the ODJB's old drummer Tony Sbarbaro.

Nick himself, in the meantime, had more immediate problems: a bout of Asian flu in 1957, recurring heart troubles, overstimulating television programs, the caprices of the Louisiana climate. In February 1958 it snowed in New Orleans for the first time in 64 years—for the first time, that is, since Nick was four years old.

> *The doctors tell me I should quit working as a carpenter. It's too much strain on my heart: I've got a dilated valve.*
> *You talk about this book like it was already published. Listen, I'll be happy to see you again, all right? Whether you get this thing published or not.*

Brass' *Story* would eventually come out, but only after a long series of rejections. Even LaRocca could not mistake the barely disguised distaste with which the book was finally received. He blamed Brass' lack of interest.

> *I could tell you weren't too interested in my last letter. Also you didn't tell me the book got rejected. What can I say, this is the kind of treatment I've come to expect in life.*

Harry Brass had just turned down a $14,000 offer from Boeing, for design and technical writing; he was working on his book full time.

He had spent that better part of 22 years on this project, paying thousands and thousands on travel and research, fighting bitterly with his mother, reaffirming his ambitions as a writer against her disapproval. Who could possibly accuse him of being lukewarm when it came to the suggestions, to the every word of his irascible dixieland god?

They say I'm crazy. They say I'm going to end up under a bridge. They're probably right. But there are things in play here that are more important than money. This book is my life's work and I intend to use every available minute and every ounce of energy on making sure, to my own satisfaction, that it's done right.

Harry's apparent coolness, his aloofness, were in fact born of prudence, of caution in handling and crystalizing the maestro's testimony. This was why, for example, he had put off transcribing one interview with the old man: he feared the naïvité of occasional collaborators might end up destroying the oracle; or that some competitor might make some duplications on the sly.

In other words, he was dealing with gold, with diamonds, with dangerous weapons when he spoke to LaRocca. Lack of interest! Brass was even running into trouble with certain civil rights groups on account of his passion: they regarded him and LaRocca alike with an infinite, fully requited distrust.

The most important task was to reassure LaRocca that the book really was going to print. Brass, in the meantime, was making the circuit of conferences in California (where he tried to interest film producers in his book), then England. But LaRocca himself remained his greatest concern. The young narrator had to explain that if this book was to see the light of day, certain affirmations and accusations—liar, communist, Jew—had to be expunged from the testimony ("whether or not it's true, Mr. LaRocca"). That sort of talk could mean the end of their deal.

Thankfully, the publishing house that had finally offered Brass a contract did not make any corrections to the manuscript. A number of New York editors had wanted the whole thing rewritten, perhaps from the perspective of Louis Armstrong's mentor, "King" Oliver. It was Brass' worst nightmare.

Finally, in April 1960, the book was out, in print. Brass set about organizing a circuit of press conferences, radio and television interviews, review copies set aside for newspapers; he booked a flight to New

Orleans for the 25th of the month with Capital Airlines, to receive such laurels as the city would bestow. He chewed his fantasy over and over like a bite of food: ten days in the town of his dreams.

The old cornetist, and his older brother Buddy, both greeted him on Constance Street, Buddy somewhat more excited than Nick. The weather was sweltering, but Harry was clammy with nerves; he did not know how LaRocca would react to hearing the cassette tapes of his news interviews, not to mention the book itself.

In one tape the interviewer, not without a touch of malice, speculated on the presence of African voodoo motifs in the ODJB's songs. It remained to be seen whether the old man could survive this without a heart attack. But after all the rages and insults, all the accusations of laziness or stupidity and all the complaints about what Brass had written or not written, the old band leader was in excellent humor. He was in the mood to laugh.

Walking home behind him—in fact, hiding behind him—the biographer saw, for the first time, the spasm in LaRocca's shoulder.

LaRocca asked to hear the recording of an interview Brass had given in Germany. What an emotion for the young man, to hear his name spoken again in German!

Before he left, Ruth LaRocca brought out cold cuts and toast. Harry's eye, always sharp, picked up the tiny insects crawling between the slices; but he thought it best not to cause trouble, and, after swallowing his repulsion, followed it with toast.

That afternoon, an invitation for a televised interview came: Jack Bear sent it. There wasn't any point throwing his pearls before a loudmouth swine like him, so Harry politely turned him down.

That same day marked the beginning of Harry's fixed routine on Bourbon Street, which ended with the inevitable evening banquet of women's flesh in the Quarter. He would start each day with an Herbsaint frappe at Sloppy Joe's, followed by breakfast at Brennan's: more Herbsaint, eggs Sardou—artichoke hearts, cream of spinach, hollandaise sauce—and perhaps a veal kidney flambé, with mushrooms and heavy cream, deglazed with brandy . . .

The bill would sometimes exceed ten dollars.

Harry's wardrobe, in the meantime, responded to the needs of the day: tan summer suits, gray tropical wool, linen the color of chocolate ice cream.

The promotion of the book was having trouble getting off the ground. General De Gaulle was in town, which threw the newspapers and television stations into a fine mess, and journalists were running about looking for French speakers to help with their op-eds. The young biographer knocked on the door at any number of empty offices that week. Night came as a relief after days so vain, and he often didn't return to his hotel before 5 o'clock.

Harry decided to decamp for Baton Rouge to see his editor. It was not an easy trip for him: the riotous nights had left him physically shaking, as if he had Alzheimer's. In the waiting room, he began to wonder what army of dancers was stomping about the inside of his skull.

The editor asked him in. Sales weren't bad, he learned; the book was in the spring bestsellers' list. Within a few more months they would probably sell 4,000 copies. Reviews were coming out, too, and even the *New York Times* had requested a copy.

Buffalo, it was confirmed, was a poor market for books. Sales there were certainly not any kind of ill omen.

The ill omen, rather, was the discovery of two enemies that Harry hadn't realized he had. One was Professor Bouchon, who had sent incandescent letters to Harry's editor, about Harry. The other was Nat Hentoff of the *Jazz Review*, which must have been some kind of beatnik journal; Harry imagined the beards with some disgust.

Back in New Orleans he made the tour of the television studios: WDSU-TV, WWL-TV, WYES-TV; then came his appointment with the *Times-Picayune*.

LaRocca had certainly warned him: nobody, nobody in that city was his friend.

It seems like wherever I go, the Maestro's bad humor stands between me and whoever I'm trying to talk to. That's the first thing that comes to their mind.

The cornetist received him at home on the torrid afternoon of April 28. He played and sang a recent composition, "Float Me Down the River to New Orleans," which Harry enjoyed. That evening, at a restaurant far too modern for Harry's tastes, they sat to a creole fish dinner, the likes of which he'd never seen: turtle soup *au sherry*, trout amandine, and Brabant potatoes. A scarlet parrot the size of an eagle greeted them at the door from its cage. Some members of a baseball team followed Harry and LaRocca, and the bird screamed "Hey there! Hi!" at them at least 50 times.

Near the parrot and its cage was a door knocker, said to bring good luck to whoever touched. Harry touched it, but the next morning when he woke up he found he'd lost $200 on the stock market. Not only that. Joe Buccia, a gentleman in his 80s who had owned a club in Storyville and whom Harry had tracked down after years of searching, hung up the phone on him: "I ain't talking to no writers."

Then, at the Steak Pit that evening, the filet was tougher than leather.

At midnight he was at WWS Radio to talk about his book. He wasn't on air until 1 o'clock, and then only for 20 minutes. Friends of the presenter wandered in and out of the studio. It was surreal. The presenter had not bothered to read a word of Harry's book. Harry sat around for another hour, speechless, waiting in vain for some listener to call in with a question: nothing. Better head back to Bourbon Street.

Sunday, the first of May, after a grapefruit juice and a glass of milk, Harry arrived at the LaRocca house. He interviewed old LaRocca on tape and then stayed for lunch. The two men ate together, facing each other across the table, while the rest of the family stayed upstairs. The LaRocca girls came in bearing the various courses, like a bevy of odalisques; Ruth, the head of the harem, had the duo pose for meticulously-snapped photos.

Afterward LaRocca played for his guest.

The next day, Brass had an appointment with the terrible Dr. Edmond Pouchon, who, over the phone, told Harry, "You won't be quite so kind to me once you've read my review of your book!"

But nothing traumatic happened. His great enemy turned out to be a refined, gracious man. They met for lunch: Brass' eyes lit up at the red beans and rice. Afterward, the great expert of New Orleans' music restrained himself to showing the younger man a long series of photographs of elderly black jazzmen, toothless and sunken-faced, without a word of commentary. After this pantomime, he took Brass for a ride in his Buick on a tour of the holy places of jazz: the ruins of Storyville, Bucktown, the Spanish Fort. Pouchon was a clumsy, distracted driver; Harry was glad to get out.

He returned to his hotel by the St. Charles streetcar. Later, at the Vieux Carré on Bourbon Street, he had a martini, followed by turtle soup *au sherry* and trout amandine.

The next morning, breakfast at Brennan's: an Herbsaint frappe and eggs Hussarde. So far, so good. The only trouble was telling the waiters apart and knowing whom to ask for what. The confusion of uniforms, from the maître d' to the busboys; the confusion of faces! He did not mean to offend anyone, still less to flatter them. He left feeling that he'd done both.

At 926 Music Street, a rundown old house, Brass spotted Emile Christian at the front door. Brass didn't get out of his taxi. They exchanged a few words through the window, just enough for the old ODJB trombonist to roar about the authorship of certain songs that LaRocca had stolen.

Under the drizzle of Wednesday, May 4, Brass saw his irascible idol for the last time. He was there for an hour. LaRocca was abrasive, bitter, in pain. Brass left for his hotel, and allowed himself to rest.

At 7 o'clock he left Room 960 of the Monteleone for a restaurant on Royal Street: a bottle of Cappelli Chianti Classico, spaghetti in tomato sauce and meatballs. Taking his leave of a city generally filled him with melancholy; but here, at least, there was always a welcome distraction to hand.

Some weeks later, Brass would write LaRocca in a panic, telling him not to speak to a certain New York television producer who wanted to make a TV version of LaRocca's story. They were trying, he wrote, to outflank him and his editor.

After all those years and thousands of dollars I spent on this, I don't have much sympathy for people who want to live off my work. I always told you that, in case of a film or TV adaptation of the book, I would split the net profits with you or with your heirs. I still hold to that and will happily sign a contract if you like. If I sell the TV rights, half the profits will go to my editor and the other half to me, according to the terms of the contract. I'd like to divide my half with you.

The cornetist wasted no time replying, astonished by the marginal role Brass wanted him to play in the use of his own life and his own biography. Yes, he had given Brass the rights for the book, but not to all the possible proceeds. Then, the promise to take care of his family was, to say the least, a joke. And anyway hadn't he spent a fortune himself, in money and in energy, on this book, on its author? He went through a long speculation on the costs of the project weighed against the earnings: a net profit for Brass, surely. How mean could Brass be, to keep LaRocca from that little sum that he deserved? Surely this wasn't all part of a strategy on Brass' part?

I should have been in on that deal with his editor myself, but I got left out. Just today I told my lawyer all about it, just to see how I fit into all this. I only want to get what I'm owed before I die for my family's sake. I appreciate the book and I thank you for the time it cost you and I'm sorry it all ended like this, on account of a misunderstanding.

CHAPTER ELEVEN

Nick (1922-1925)

Once he'd recovered from his pneumonia, LaRocca managed to reconvene his band, with a few substitutions. On April 10, 1922 they played the Flatbush Theater in Brooklyn. In May they played Coney Island, and spent the rest of the summer there.

In this period, in the afternoons, LaRocca and Edwards had taken to fishing, a calming and profitable way to wake up after sleeping through the morning. They acquired a motorboat some 18 feet long, and they'd chug up the Hudson in it, along the Palisades toward Poughkeepsie.

I think I'm the first one ever to take lobster in Sheepshead Bay. I put traps out with fish heads in them. Edwards was a better fisherman than me, but he couldn't take shellfish like I could. I was taking about a dozen lobster a night those days. The dustman saw all the shells and couldn't figure out how we could afford it all. It took him a few weeks to realize I was sneaking out about two in the morning to pick up my traps, and then my secret was blown.

The anti-jazz movement that year didn't manage to ruin the ODJB. It was too late for that: the band's prestige was too well-established. Their music, which spread with sales of the phonograph, brought an air of bootlegging with it, of uninhibited dancing and sex. Its enemies were relentless. They called it pathological, neurotic, degrading, lewd, even pagan. Religious figures, civil authorities, and various *bien pensants* came together to declare jazz and jazz dancing immoral and degenerate, and in some cases they banned it outright.

In December 1922 LaRocca signed with the OKeh Phonograph Corporation to cut some new records. He wanted to add a saxophone, by now the emblem of jazz, to the group. It was not a happy decision. The saxophone tamed the old dixieland style, sweetening it into syrup.

LaRocca broke the OKeh contract in a rage when he learned that the new 78s were being sold as "race records"—music, that is, for a black audience.

In April 1923 the ODJB toured New England, quickly returning to Broadway when an impresario pointed a pistol at LaRocca and suggested he give up any hope of a pay raise, however big the crowds might be at their shows. In the winter of 1923-24 they played again at the Balconades. There, LaRocca met "Bix" Beiderbecke, a youth with two loves in his life: the ODJB and hard liquor.

Bix's fate was sealed from the moment the trill of LaRocca's cornet reached his ears. He went out and got a cornet of his own and tried, by playing along with the records, to reproduce Nick's solos. Thus the first pieces in Bix's repertoire were old dixieland classics: "Tiger Rag," "At the Jazz Band Ball," "Bluin' the Blues," "Ostrich Walk"... He was still in high school then. It was a great day for him with the Dixelanders stopped in Davenport, of all places, for a show.

"He followed us down the street," remembers LaRocca, "just to get a look at us. He couldn't believe that we were just normal guys. Then he asked me to play a couple notes for him, and I said sure, why not."

But by 1923 it was Paul Whiteman, not Nick LaRocca, who formed the public taste. Jazz pieces for dancing were out; easy, mellow tunes were selling. Clarinets and trombones disappeared from the orchestras, replaced by violins and guitars. The trumpets were invariably muted.

The cornetist lived lavishly, recklessly. More and more he argued with his irreverent and undisciplined trombonist, Eddie Edwards.

LaRocca wore two-hundred-dollar suits fashioned by Manhattan's smartest tailor and diamond rings that sparkled in the glaring lights of nocturnal Broadway. In the afternoon he could be seen heading for Long Island in his fire-engine-red Stutz Bearcat. On the Long Island Speedway you could pay a dollar for the privilege of driving as fast as you liked, and LaRocca, garbed in goggles and duster, with his cap fitted backwards, tried to make his Bearcat fly.

By January 1925, LaRocca suffered a nervous breakdown. His doctor encouraged him to give up his fast living. He considered this advice, then packed his belongings into one of his cars, a '23 Buick sedan, and left New York heading south. He drove like he was drugged, wandering aimlessly and without any sense of orientation, and wouldn't arrive in New Orleans for some weeks.

And to think of all the money I lost between '18 and '36! I was sick when I left New York, I didn't thinking I was leaving anything valuable behind—just the Stutz roadster, which I planned to sell to a garage on 145th Street. I got a quote for it in the mail, but then the garage changed owner. That was the last I heard of it.

CHAPTER TWELVE

Harry (1960-1962)

A score of newspapers and magazines from around the world had reviewed Harry's book. The reception was general, swift and harsh:

> *This is the rather idolatrous story of five musicians from New Orleans, known to hobbyists as the O.D.J.B. It tells the history of jazz from the point of view of Nick LaRocca . . . Perhaps he wishes things took place that way, but . . . Most dubious of all is the assertion that the Original Dixieland Jazz Band "invented" jazz in Chicago around 1916. Nowhere does the book mention the role of Negroes . . . As Louis Armstrong said, all they did was copy the music that they heard negroes playing in New Orleans. As far as Mr. Brass is concerned Armstrong adds, "There's no truth in him."*

Satchmo—who had written in *Swing that Music* that "the first great jazz orchestra was formed in New Orleans by a cornet player named Dominick James LaRocca"—was apparently disappointed that Buddy Bolden, Freddie Keppard, "Kid" Ory and other black and creole jazzmen made no appearance in Harry's book.

None of these arguments were new to Brass and none of them held much weight for him. It was further proof, he thought grimly, that he and his idol were unloved in the world. He tried to focus on the positive side of the *querelle*: all publicity, he sighed, was good publicity.

He focused instead on his European lecture circuit—but only after dashing off a memo to his detractors on stationary stamped, in blue and gold, with the words "ORIGINAL DIXIELAND JAZZ BAND—THE CREATORS OF JAZZ—AUTHORIZED HISTORIAN:"

> *I'm afraid that of the two of us it's you, not me, who wants these racial polemics. As a musician, I've always held*

that jazz transcends all questions of color or creed.

Brass even thought an essay, for a journal called *Jazz and Politics*, would puncture the common assumption that jazz was black music from its birth. But music writers were liberals, he considered, even extremists; they'd have nothing to do with it.

The ODJB, in the meantime, had been cast out of the official histories of jazz.

But the arguments went on. One argument: LaRocca's band had the privilege of cutting the first jazz record not because they were particularly good, but because they were white, and the record companies wanted white bands. Another: historians had no right to sneer at the anti-Italian discrimination that was general in New Orleans at the time.

A third: that Brass' book was just a hodge-podge of anecdotes and banalities, an amateur's hobbyhorse, not worth the trouble of serious readers.

This third and least just opinion sped an anxious Harry Brass to England in February 1962 to begin his conference circuit. He stayed with a friend of his, a music critic, in Hatch End. He'd no sooner arrived than he came down with a sore throat, which his friend's wife treated with honey and lemon juice. But what frightened the debutant conference-giver was not his throat: it was a strike at the Coventry Jaguar plant. He would have to put off buying his next car. The London office told him there was nothing to be done; for a fee of five pounds he could have a car delivered to his friend's house in Hatch End. Brass didn't miss this opportunity, but it ate him inside not to be able to receive his new car right at the place where it was born. But it was the only way around the strike, and in any case it meant no traffic jams and no driving while under the weather.

The secretary who arranged the delivery warned him repeatedly to drive the new Jaguar cautiously, adding with what sounded like a smile that only he should have the right to destroy his own Jaguars.

After lunch with his hosts, Chris and Mary and their little girl, Brass helped prepare marmalade, peeling and slicing oranges. He was not to throw away the seeds, they told him; and they showed him what to do with the little white mountain on the table.

Later Brass received visitors: five jazz musicians, devotees of the ODJB, who all lived together in one minibus to save money. They were to play at the official release of the British edition of his book, with the press present. Mary served the six disciples a dish of pork, burnt to the color of ebony. British discretion was observed.

The next day the Jaguar was to arrive. After lunch, Brass sat like a statue by the living room window, anxious to see his new beauty. She arrived on Grimsdyke Road at exactly three. Harry ran out to admire her, pulsing with joy.

The driver who had brought it out from London was courteous, almost fawning; he demonstrated the various buttons and gauges of the car, capping every sentence with a "sir," and then brought out the documents to be signed. Then there were more documents to sign, and more after that; Harry was afraid he'd have to swear eternal love to the Queen before they let him have his car. But perhaps it was only impatience.

The test drive went poorly. The Jaguar employee sat up front with Harry. "You see, sir, you're driving the wrong way," he said, ever the bland and courteous navigator. The curious swarmed to see him pass, pressing into windows; even the buses slowed down to watch that little white marvel with the red interior go by. A lorry driver called out, asking if he wanted to trade.

Harry spent the rest of the day poring over the owner's manual, marveling at the latest innovations: the windows, the steering wheel, the ventilator.

The English plate number was 693-WK.

The next day, at the Ken Coyler Club in Covent Garden, Brass went to present his book. The club was below street level, and freezing, unheated; he awaited the press wrapped up in his overcoat, shivering violently. A pile of his books sat on a small table.

An hour passed; no one came. The agent who had booked the affair, a certain Jackson, hadn't bothered to come either. An incompetent. His exasperation was mounting, and although he'd managed to avoid it until now, he gave up and sat at the bar. The double gin and tonic went down in a gulp. The party was over. Three spectators and a pair of music critics, who in any event had come late. The release could not have been more miserable if he'd planned it to be.

The ODJB cover band stayed on to insist that Harry be their agent on some upcoming tour of the United States. One more waste of time; one more public humiliation.

Harry mulled the failure for a long time, searching for a reason why and turning up nothing. He passed the evening with a new friend in Soho's red-light district: a redhead from Finland named Heli, 19 years old. She was a dancer at the Venus Room. She'd come to London to work as a waitress, but her looks had landed her here, doing striptease.

Harry appointed Heli as his steady companion for his three weeks in England. He took the train in to London almost every day to see her. Between the girl's acts, the two would go dancing, or order steaks and champagne and beaujolais at Soho's French bistros; the bill often made him shudder.

One afternoon, when they were out walking, Harry pointed out to her the snowdrops that were beginning to press out of the winter soil, a sign of spring. As if invited, his Finnish *soubrette* launched into the squalid story of her life until now, from Finland to her present condition. Harry was disconcerted by her frankness; he would have preferred a bouquet of easy, inoffensive lies.

The last time they met, the writer gave her an elegant cigarette holder, which suited her desire to at least play at being an aristo, if she couldn't be the real thing. Then they dined at an Indian restaurant, and afterward drank enough martinis to drown their little story forever.

Mr. Brass, I'm sorry to see that all you do is complain about how much this book costs. Did you want me to reimburse you? I appreciate your work and I know you had a lot of troubles getting it done but there were plenty of others who wanted to write this book. I turned them down because I gave you my word. You're going to have author rights for many years. You say the sales are slow, well that's not what they're telling me! This book is going to have a long life even after I'm dead and gone. But I'm reserving the rights to tell my story for myself and my heirs.

You sent me a contract that I was supposed to sign which gave you absolute rights. I'm not a lawyer but I wish I was right now, because I

NEVER gave up those rights and if I did it would be illegal anyway.

Two things remained before Harry's tour of Norway: a final conference in Coventry, and sending the car back to Buffalo. A quiet little man in black came to pick him up the car Hatch End, with a copy of Harry's invoice:

REF 2472 - LONDON/NEW YORK - 21022 MR BRASS - JAGUAR TYPE E - WE ARE PLEASED TO CONFIRM TO MR BRASS THAT THE PRICE WILL REMAIN AT $235 TO TRANSPORT HIS AUTO FROM LONDON TO NEW YORK - CONVEY PARIS.

The man began a detailed inventory of all the accessories that might be damaged or stolen in transit, and Harry begged him, again and again, to be careful driving it in the lorry, and to avoid third gear.

As far as the Coventry lecture went, he boarded his train bored and irritated. He felt like he was wasting his last hours in England. He would have to change trains at Watford Junction and then take a taxi.

What had drawn Harry to this conference, as that incompetent of his agent had explained it, was the fact that he would be entrusting himself to the local intelligentsia. In this case, he was to arrive at the conference site and wait for "two gentlemen in hats."

It was a spy novel atmosphere, in short, and at the appointed hour Harry was pacing the lobby of the hotel darkly, his own hat pulled down. The hotel was freezing inside.

The meeting with the organizers turned out to be cordial enough. Harry avoided all the polemics about race with care: one of the organizers introduced his wife, a dark young woman from Trinidad. Surely a progressive, thought Harry.

There were more people than chairs in the conference hall. Brass spoke for two hours or more and never seemed to lose the crowd: the famous English phlegm, he thought, although he reflected that during his last days with Chris and Mary, they had stopped trying to hide how insufferable they found him.

Brass would even sell the five copies of his book that he'd brought with him on tour.

Most everyone in the media sympathizes with the Left. The extremists of them, the bleeding hearts, are fixated on the "poor, oppressed Negroes." It's an obsession. Unfortunately, just about all the jazz writers are part of this category too. They want to give the Negroes the exclusive honor of having invented jazz. Well. This is where this legend comes from, the jazz was born in Africa and the white man took it away or whatever.

Norway was a revelation. It was supposed to be the second stop on Brass' European tour; he made it his endpoint. Oslo had snared him like a thrush in birdlime. He canceled the rest of his tour and dedicated the next few months to the girls of Oslo, where, in the years to come, he would come back a dozen times.

CHAPTER THIRTEEN

Nick (1936-1938)

In the ten years after his breakdown, the cornetist of the ODJB concentrated all of his energies on construction and electrical installations. With his own hands and minimal help from some of the boys in the neighborhood, he built a number of houses around New Orleans, including a few for himself. He also helped demolish some houses too run down to renovate.

He had no will at all to revisit his dixieland days, and no reason to.

The boys from the band had dispersed. A few had tried to revive the name and the repertoire, without much success. Between Edwards and Sbarbaro, LaRocca preferred the latter as successor. But it didn't really matter. The jazz scene had been occupied, as it were, by the symphonic arrangements of Paul Whiteman, protagonist of the 1933 film *The King of Jazz*.

But then the radio happened, and so did Benny Goodman, and people began dusting off their old disks. Bits of old ODJB still occasionally ended up on the radio. Goodman, the "King of Swing," was frank about his admiration of the style, exciting if somewhat *d'antan*, of the ODJB's Larry Shields.

"I was playing jazz on my clarinet when I was eight years old, listening to the records of the Original Dixieland Jazz Band, which made a terrific impression on me..."

A certain theatrical impresario also helped reawaken the public's dormant memories of the band from New Orleans. In the mid 1930s, he had the idea of reuniting the group for a film a musical. Joseph Russel Robinson, the old ODJB pianist, tried to convince Nick LaRocca. It didn't work. Carpentry was easier; it was all he wanted to do.

LaRocca noticed, however, that even after ten years the world still remembered the old Original Dixieland Jazz Band. Turning the matter over in his mind, his conviction grew that his role, in the history of jazz, was something special, something unique.

One day, without warning, the 50-year-old ex-musician decided to hang up his clawhammer and trowel and look up Larry Shields, whose style had made the most obvious impact on swing music. He traced him to a bible society in New Orleans. Shields' hair looked like a white helmet. He hadn't touched his clarinet in ten years.

On May 19, 1936 the two made an appearance at the Old Absinthe House on Bourbon Street.

Boys and girls THAT was swing music...just a trumpet and clarinet... but how those boys went to town. Maybe they have had a twelve-year layoff...but you'd never believe it listening to 'em...and you should have heard the storm of applause they provoked from the pop-eyed audience... pop-eyed because they couldn't believe that a white-haired grandpop like Larry could make that clarinet screech, wail and sob as it was doing.... or how that left-handed trumpeter could get such a seductive swing into the rhythm as Nick was doing.

The two old musicians wanted to be sure, above all, that they still had it, that they still had the lungs for it, rusty or not.

LaRocca, not without considerable resistance and innumerable letters in the mail, managed to reconquer Edwards, Robinson and Sbarbaro. The trombonist suffered from a swollen lip, but he was the most impatient to make people dance again, to play again the music of his youth.

They began practicing in earnest, so intensely that one night LaRocca fell asleep while driving home and crashed into a tree, somehow surviving uninjured.

The evening of July 28, 1936, the band debuted on an NBC Red Network broadcast. They didn't play very long. The overture was "Margie;" the finale, "Tiger Rag." Offers for engagements began coming in the next day.

LaRocca insisted on expanding the group by nine, in order to meet the new standards of the symphonic, swing era. The old veterans would take the solos. Edwards quit, but the band did grow: four saxophones, four trumpets (including the leader), two trombones, a piano, a guitar, a double bass, and drums. On September 2 and September 9, 1936, this group cut a record for Victor; later, a second disk would pair them with Benny Goodman: "Clarinet Marmalade" on the A side, "St. Louis Blues" on the B side.

"Nick, you boys have still got something nobody else has got."

A quarrel about money in the summer of 1936 saw Larry Shields withdraw, if only briefly. LaRocca got him back by the end of the year. On January 6, 1937 the original core of the ODJB played the RKO Boston Theatre; then Chicago, Memphis, New Orleans. A month later Louis de Rochemont dedicated his episode of *March of Time* to them.

New fame brought new quarrels, however, quarrels over money. LaRocca—who had fronted the initial investments and signed all the contracts in the name of the group—was dividing the profits into six parts, one for each man plus two for himself. This, plus his registration of songs solely under his own name, lead to resentment and tension.

The cornetist was in no position to put out these smoldering tensions. He was getting mixed up in an editorial enterprise at the same time, with Robinson. Edwards, Sbarbero and Shields were furious. One night in Cincinnati the three of them walked out on LaRocca just before the curtain went up, leaving him to play, alone and humiliated, on an empty stage.

In spite of all this, on March 15, 1937 LaRocca married the 18-year-old Ruth Dorothy Pitre of Thibodaux, Louisiana. He was 48. They would have six children together: James in 1940, Ruth in 1942, Dominic, Jr. in 1943, Jerome in 1944, Carol Louise in 1946, and Carl Louis in 1952.

On April 21, 1937, the band started a two week gig at the Silver Grill in Buffalo.

While the others bustled around the stage before a show, Sbarbaro would drink and begin raving about the high times they'd had in 1917, when he'd have to drive hundreds of miles up muddy roads just to hear the Original Dixieland Jazz Band. Twenty years had passed. He was moved; he remembered the teddy bear he used to keep with his drum kit.

The next few months saw a war of attrition, a war of nerves, break out between LaRocca on the one side and Edwards and Shields on the other. They laid ambushes for him: one night they pointed their instruments down in just such a way that the only sound the audience could hear was the cornet. Other plots, other little mutinies followed. A strange letter came from the musicians' union, addressed to LaRocca; then someone broke into his car, taking records and sheet music. On the night of January 17, 1938, at the RKO Palace Theatre in Chicago, LaRocca had had enough of the tension and the sneers of his bandmates. He sat down to write that they were closing shop.

Palace Theater Chicago, Ill. Gentlemen:—After the completion of the present engagements with Ken Murray, I hereby give notice that the Original Dixieland Jazz Band will be disbanded. I am very sorry to have to come to this conclusion, but owing to the internal friction, which makes it impossible to carry on, I am mailing a copy of this notice to Local #802. Very truly yours, D. Jas. LaRocca, Leader and Re-organizer Original Dixieland Jazz Band

On the first of February, 1938, the band had ceased to exist.

Edwards, Shields and Sbarbaro attempted to revive the band, bringing on Sharkey Bonanno on the trumpet and Frank Signorelli on keys. This arrangement lasted until 1940. A final attempt by Edwards and Sbarbaro foundered in 1943.

CHAPTER FOURTEEN

Harry (1962-1963)

On December 5, 1961 Harry boarded the MS *Bergensfjord,* which crossed back and forth between the States and Norway every week. He didn't know that every year, a great number of Norwegian girls would take that very ship back home from New York to celebrate Christmas at home.

The ship, in other words, was a bedlam of girls, and the well-dressed American quickly found himself invited to the many little impromptu parties they threw. By the time he set foot back in Europe he could claim to have made some friends; he had no idea, however, how many times he would end up repeating this trip.

That Christmas he stayed at the Sjusjøen Høyfjellshotell, in a ski resort north of Oslo. His plans to give a couple talks in that city of women came to a rather dishonorable end, indefinitely postponed. The pretty girls there were endless but stupid; Harry suffered through their musical ignorance, their taste for cheap costume jewelry, their easy virtue in matters of love.

He often found himself coming back to his hotel room sunk in depression. In the mornings he took long walks to ward it off, followed by grandiose breakfasts that cost him 15 kroner. Otherwise he lay in bed, listening to classical music on the radio and drinking beer.

One day he ran into Arut Christiansen, an old businessman who had made deals with the Brass' father once, and who seemed to know everyone in Norway: "Would you like to meet King Olaf? Princess Margarethe? The prime minister maybe?" he asked Brass foxily at a New Year's concert. "Or perhaps you'd prefer Miss Norway, eh?"

Harry nodded at what he thought was another of the old man's little jokes. But Arut seized him by the arm and dragged him to a blonde of 20, Ragnhild, who'd come sixth at the Miss Universe pageant of 1960 in Florida. She was gazing at her young admirers with magnificent disdain.

The old man sat Harry down with her at a table in the saloon. Harry remembered her from a television interview. She did not believe him. He remembered her saying that she rather liked American men. It went on like this until Arut rejoined them, and they all drank a beer and sang together.

That night Brass called her a taxi and accompanied her home.

Three days later they saw each other again: in the end she had accepted his invitation to dinner. She had bobbed her hair in the meantime, but she was bewitching that night, more radiant than when he first met her. Even the busiest passersby found themselves vaguely perturbed at the sight of her.

Harry had beef stroganoff, while Ragnhild limited herself to bread and fruit. Then, after a half hour of playing the gracious hostess, she sent him home. She had, she said, a work meeting to attend.

No, it wouldn't be Ragnhild after all who got Harry stuck in Oslo. That would be Inger, a 19-year-old English student, who spoke both of Norway's languages and could not resist Harry's manners or his repeated invitations to Blom's, where she tasted her first cocktail, an Orange Blossom, and ate beef stroganoff with him.

As the girl had to get home before late, Harry continued the evening at the Metropol, between music and new acquaintances.

In his role as authorized historian of the ODJB, Harry did almost nothing in Oslo, apart from meeting with the music critic of the *Aftenposten*.

The idyll with Inger started on January 17, 1962 in Dovrehallen, a discotheque frequented by students, which was packed that evening; Harry could only get in by pretending to be a journalist investigating a story. A full 24 years separated the couple, but they danced as if at the Capulets' ball. A series of dates followed: movies, jazz shows, dinners out, and eventually more intimate appointments than these at the Hotel Viking.

Three months had gone by like this, or more, when the gallant had to return to America; his parents had threatened to cut off his bank account access if he didn't.

It's not a particularly trustworthy book, unfortunately.

A few months later, Harry was forced to assume the inauspicious role of stateside manager for the fanatical English ODJB cover band. They toured as the "Original Downtown Syncopators," and promoted the "Nick LaRocca Dixieland Jazz Club" at the shows. Harry had become their manager during a meeting at the office of an important impresario, without ever managing to get a word in on his own behalf. He walked out of the office patron of the band.

He arranged a dozen shows for them around the East Coast: Buffalo, Cleveland, Philadelphia, New York. The band arrived in Buffalo on October 9, 1962, to considerable publicity from the tourism offices and chambers of commerce of the towns on their itinerary. At the Buffalo airport, in fact, a dance troupe of local girls awaited them in the terminal. It was a royal welcome, in short, and the boys were clearly more at their ease than they had been in the minibus they'd shared in England, with its red and white Ivy League stripes. At their side now was the impeccable Harry Brass, whom they dragged to their first few shows. Within days, however, they left Harry to his own embarrassment and began organizing concerts without him. He would have been grateful, except they also left him out of the fee negotiations, which irritated him to no end.

Even though I've earned a few thousand in royalties in the two years since publication, it wasn't even enough to cover my travel expenses. That's not even counting the expenses accrued in Europe. Hotels, photographers, phone calls, disks... My income in those years was zero dollars: everything went into fees and taxes. The only real, long term effect of my book was the general recognition of my role as historian of the ODJB.

Harry went back to Oslo in December to see Inger, with whom he'd kept up a busy correspondence. Even her parents seemed to approve of him; they often asked him to dinner. But one night after they'd eaten, when Harry coughed out a marriage proposal, Inger said no. Harry left. They picked up their correspondence again, but this time her parents started intercepting the letters.

He came again to Norway many times in those years, until Inger finally told him she was no longer in love with him.

The news came in a long letter with meticulous expressions of gratitude, not only on her part but her family's: he'd given her a necklace, records, a pocketbook in green leather, a hat, expensive cheeses, Christmas cards. She listed them over the course of seven or eight pages. Finally she came to the point, that the affair was over and might Harry be so kind and so gallant as to quietly disappear, to stop writing her and stop calling. Her new beau would appreciate it. She closed with a delicate, irrevocable adieu.

About 30 years later, in 1994, Harry would stop by the office in Oslo where he'd learned that Inger worked as a secretary, just to say hello.

You see, I liked that Nick LaRocca and the ODJB were insulted endlessly by the jazz writers, accused of plagiarism, accused of racism, of rigidity in their rhythms, of boring tempos, of uninspired improvisations, of vulgarity. I'm here to prove them all wrong!

CHAPTER FIFTEEN

Nick (until February 22, 1961)

In 1943, when the copyrights on the ODJB's compositions were due to expire, LaRocca renewed them with such alacrity that it opened all the half-healed wounds among the former bandmates. Their rancor over LaRocca's unjust monopoly of the authorship rights boiled back into life.

The cornetist had endorsed Larry Shields' membership in the American Society of Composers, Authors and Publishers, but hadn't responded to Eddie Edwards' or Tony Spargo (né Sbarbaro)'s request for a recommendation. Neither of them would see any royalties from "Tiger Rag," "Sensation Rag," or "Mournin' Blues."

An episode of the CBS program *You Are There*, broadcast in the early 1950s, dismissed the ODJB as thieves and liars for having taken "Tiger Rag" from Jelly Roll Morton. Edwards and Shields took the broadcaster to court and won a handsome settlement.

LaRocca had been 48 when he declared the Original Dixieland Jazz Band dissolved for the last time. He had just gotten married and already had a daughter, and considered his time better spent on other things than memories of his band or responding to the various lies and accusations that people threw at it. He would pick that up much later, when he was 65 and had enough money in the bank to do it properly. He didn't hold back. His letters and photocopies circulated the globe.

His garage, in this period, had become his personal archive and a refuge from his enemies. His copy machine and typewriter were his artillery. His prose sometimes suffered from indifferent grammar, but musicians, critics, jazz club owners, and even well-known journalists would manage to decipher it.

August 3, 1958 marked the first shots of his counteroffensive. The *Times-Picayune* had received one of the cornetist's missives, and dedicated several inches of print to disproving them. Others leaped into the fight. Even Phil Napoleon contributed, with an open letter recognizing LaRocca and his colleagues' role in bringing jazz out of the dives and whorehouses and into the most refined clubs in the world.

The pugnacious old cornetist, in the midst of all this chaos, kept composing new songs, which his son Jimmy transcribed as sheet music: "Swamp Water Ballad," "Irish Channel Drag," "Down in Old New Orleans," "Let's Jam It," "You Name It," "Now Everybody Step," "Is It True."

He even took risks on waltzes and ballades, sometimes inspired by works of poetry.

. . . it's well known that the Ford Foundation was run by communists and backed the Negroes. That all came out in front of Congress years ago.

The time had come to damn one's soul if necessary—and this held for LaRocca and his biographer—to seize some permanent spot in the history that jazz was amassing around itself. One had to speak, to shout, to document, to fight. It was not enough to secure four or five lines buried in an encyclopedia, or a couple condescending citations in some history of 20th-century music. One had to muscle through. One had to fill in spaces in the truth if necessary; in any case a fib here or there certainly wouldn't invalidate the point of the story. This battle, especially after the *Story of the Original Dixieland Jazz Band* was published, required precise, watertight arguments, and as little contradiction as possible.

LaRocca did not leave the fight to others. If his biographer had overlooked the first stirrings of jazz among black musicians, it must have been a strategic choice, to limit the book's potential for historical controversy. After all, the book was about the ODJB; and anyway, in LaRocca's view it was the white man who faced racism and ostracism in the history of jazz, on account of the color of his skin. He himself had been further penalized, he said, because he was from the South, and worse, an Italian.

Look, if I said colored guys didn't contribute to jazz I'd be telling you a lie. They contributed as much as the white man, all right? But they didn't have a model to get started with. The ODJB was the prototype and everyone else imitated us. Take that record of Louis Armstrong, Sweet Little Papa, *and listen to "Ostrich Walk." They stole it from us. Louis came nine years after us; we were his model.*

He denied the version of the story that held black groups to have been discriminated against, "ghettoized," by the record companies and nightclub owners. A lot of them were playing the big clubs in New Orleans and New York, even before the ODJB debuted on Broadway. King Oliver and Johnny Dodds and Armstrong came later.

LaRocca's enemies ("liars, all of them") even claimed that he had tampered with the original Reisenweber's contract of March 25, 1918, sending around falsified photocopies that made him look like the only player in the ODJB who counted.

Grasping desperately at any chance of lasting glory, Nick LaRocca did not hesitate to change the amount of money each musician received in the contract, nor to write his own name over that of Max Hart or Edwin Edwards, the latter being responsible for business relations for the Original Dixieland Jazz Band at that time.

When one researcher asked him to clarify who exactly wrote the "Original Dixieland One-Step," LaRocca replied, with an ambiguous smile, that it could only be one of his own, given that he was still receiving a third of the royalties for it.

It was something of an Ubu Roi *response by this man of passion and excess, inclined toward blending truth and lies, obsessively jealous and obsessed with defending "his" Original Dixieland Jazz Band.*

LaRocca was said (not always with admiration) to have picked up early on the power of public relations. His tenacious reiteration of his story spread and reinforced a kind of fake truth—widely believed, too, not least by the "ears that would believe anything" of the ODJB's "authorized historian."

He held the cornet with his right hand and used his left on the valves,
the reverse of his peers. LaRocca may or may not have been the best white
cornetist in New Orleans at the time, but he had a rarer quality than
that: huge ambition, matched by an instinct to seize the day. He seemed
to be the only one in his circles who could really took advantage of the
situations in which they found themselves. Indeed, no other band ever
benefited from such a series of happy circumstances.

One of the most biting charges pressed against LaRocca was that
he had publicly proclaimed himself the creator of jazz. But he wasn't
the only one. Jelly Roll Morton had, too; so had Clarence Williams,
the cornetist Buddy Bolden . . . Authentic pioneers, or clever imitators?

A number of their records from the period between 1917 and '22
demonstrate that the ODJB had little to learn from the famous Creole
Jazz Band, formed in 1923 by King Oliver, and still less from Kid Ory's
handful of recordings from 1921. LaRocca's technique was superior to Ory's
and his phrasing [...] was second to none of the black trumpeters of the era.

One day in 1958, when he was almost 70 and still working in
construction, LaRocca had to be rushed to the hospital. The doctors
diagnosed angina pectoris and kept him overnight.

Domenic James LaRocca died at 3:40pm on February 22, 1961,
at his house at 2218 Constance Street, the one he'd built himself.
He'd been sitting in the armchair that had belonged to the mother
of his young wife.

Ruth had borne six children by Nick, not counting one born
before, and remained in his house for another half century. Inscribed
over the front door are the notes to the refrain of "Tiger Rag."

Before long, Ruth LaRocca had about 20 grandchildren and
ten or so great-grandchildren. She guarded her late husband's final
compositions, the ones he'd written for her, with appropriate jealousy.

Of their children, Carol plays the piano and the clarinet. James
is a trumpeter. Carl studied music formally. Ruth has a lovely singing
voice. The grandchildren often play for their grandmother.

Nick LaRocca's archives were donated to Tulane University. Nearby, at the New Orleans Jazz Museum, stands a bronze bust of him, made in 1999 by the Sicilian sculptor Disma Tumminello.

I met him by the waterfront, in New Orleans. I didn't know who he was. When the music started, I saw him walking through the crowd; Nick really knew everyone. He asked me if I wanted to dance. I said yes. He really was a very good dancer. Then he asked, "Can I have the next dance?" I said no; I don't really know why. Anyway that was our first meeting. It was 1936. He was about to leave, for Texas I think, but when he came back he called me.

Travel had lost its luster for Nick during his years of frenetic touring; in any event, he had difficulty with airplanes. His one trip to Sicily would have been around the time his youngest sister, Mary, was born, according to Ruth; and Nick didn't speak Italian.

Before they had children Nick and Ruth used to picnic by the Mississippi whenever they could. They'd stop the car on the way for Italian bread and Italian cheese. Nick was an excellent cook but he detested spaghetti. He liked wine. He liked to enjoy himself.

When Tulane asked Ruth for Nick's first cornet she refused. That was to go to her son, James.

In Nick LaRocca's formative years, 1910 to 1912, the Eagle Band, Oscar "Papa" Celestin, Johnson, Oliver, Keppard, Tig Chambers and Manuel Perez were all playing in Storyville. It's hard to believe LaRocca never heard any of these great pioneers.

In the months before his death he made several unexpected and frankly incredible gestures of affection and confidence toward his beleaguered biographer. Without him, his "best friend," the book could never have been written. He was calculating, in 24 years, his own period of crucifixion.

What distinguished the Original Dixieland Jazz Band from other groups was its soaring passion, its ability to play faster and wilder than anyone was used to. No one had ever heard anything as frenetic, as alive, as the ODJB. Their music resonated physically in the listener, almost viscerally.

At the Greenwood Cemetery of New Orleans, in a marble chapel distinguished by its florid elegance and under a little stone cross, an inscription reaffirms the cornetist's lifelong cry:

Beloved husband of Ruth Pitre. April 11, 1889 – Feb. 22, 1961. Here lies the world's first man in jazz.

CHAPTER SIXTEEN

Harry (today)

His weekly shopping run, by taxi, and the stairs up to the third floor can lay Harry out for the rest of the day. If he runs through the roster of his friends, the ones his own age, he can't think of any who are left. When he feels like he can't go on he calls 911, and the paramedics wheel him into the emergency room of the VA hospital. It's a valve of his heart, that trombone of an organ without any breath behind it. A transplant would be a serious risk for a man past 80, as Harry well knows.

He crashed his Mazda truck some years ago, but Harry is still astounded by the fact that he no longer has his own means to get around—he who had lived for his cars.

A number of books on his shelf come from a Sicilian correspondent, beside a number of books about Sicily: Durrell's *Sicilian Carousel*, Mary Taylor Smith's *Island of Persephone*, Daphne Phelps' *A House in Sicily*.

Please feel free to ask about anything, any subject that interests you . . .

He still occasionally paints with oils, mostly landscapes. He takes green tea every morning and afternoon for his health. After dinner, he moves on to a series of little pours of vodka.

His brother James, older by ten years, a retired mechanical engineer, lives in North Carolina. The classic fight over their parents' will has kept them from talking for 20 years. His other brother, William, was a celebrated veterinarian at the Ambassador Animal Hospital outside Washington, DC. He counted among his patients Jimmy Roosevelt's cat, General Mark Clark's dog, and Ethel Kennedy's monkey. William, seven years younger than Harry, had been executor of Harry's will: archives, records, books, film, paintings, bank accounts, investments, everything.

After my death, he must come live in Amherst until all my affairs are sorted.

Recently, Louisiana State University Press has accepted Brass' proposal for a new edition of the *Story of the Original Dixieland Jazz Band.* They may change the title: *From Jas to Jazz,* perhaps. Harry would like to add a new chapter about his friend, the comedian Jimmy Durante, who had died in 1980. Durante was more than a big nose: he was another forerunner of jazz and an imitator of the ODJB.

As in the previous editions of the book, the text should remain unaltered. A couple new chapters will explore the cornetist's character at greater depth.

LaRocca's grammar and spelling were terrible. He'd undergone an operation on one of his eyes, too, which affected his sight and caused all kinds of errors when he typed. He didn't use much punctuation and his sentences would run into each other, without any syntax at all. I got used to all that and could always translate it, but it might give you some trouble.

Harry needs about six months to complete the new writing, by his own reckoning. He can't write more than a few hours a day: his health won't permit it. This time, there won't be a raging Nick LaRocca to receive the final piece, waving a 23-year-old letter in his face, written by a naive, 18-year-old Harry, who had offered to split all profits from the book evenly.

He was disappointed by the book. He complained that I'd washed all the color out of him as a person. He was right, of course. The editors had reduced the book drastically, and there wasn't much I could do about it.

When Harry, to help his flagging memory, picked up his old diaries again and relived the ancient love affairs that still weighed on his flabby shoulders, he remembered that his brief engagement in 1950 had left him so despondent that he had neither the will, nor the emotional means, to avoid the endless misadventures in love that followed.

He looked at that one line, written by hand, the ink disappearing into the paper . . .

Joy, his disastrous first love, lived in a house of the general proportions and appearance of an antique ocean liner. Her father had been the major shareholder in the firm that built the bridges of the New York State Thruway between Buffalo and Albany. Millions of dollars passed under those bridges. Harry's mother and Joy's mother had been classmates in school, and later members of the Amherst Community Church.

Harry's diary has nothing to say about those months, those days. There had been a grand engagement party, with hundreds of guest and valet parking.

She was an amateur actress, Joy, and she managed to co-opt Harry into her theater group. They called him Jack Benny. His attempts at acting and writing musical comedies didn't lead anywhere. He himself called his contributions to little productions of *Mr. Barry's Etchings, Star Gazing, Maid in Manhattan,* and *Time for Elizabeth* "questionable." But he stayed in the Amherst Players after he broke up with Joy. Their story had been a continuous, asymmetrical fight. She was neurotic, impulsive, aggressive; he was apathetic, passive, unable to fight back.

All that Harry now remembers of that year is what he called his "pride and joy:" his car, a sumptuous yellow '37 Cord convertible.

Nothing good ever came of this not for me or my family, just problems. I think I would have been better off without your book because I needed calm and rest. But how could I have let them write about me this way the way they wrote about your book? I want to be your friend Mr. Brass and I'll help you as best I can with these new chapter, but its too late to start thinking about fixing things up over leaving out the negroes from those early years.

There was, however, another love affair in 1958, with a wicked redhead named Carol, which Harry now remembers as "the most devastating" of his life. Her hair was scarlet, flaming, says Harry. Even her eyes were red. He had met her at a party in the basement flat she shared with two other girls, all airline hostesses. They were together three months, three months as long and intense as a lifetime.

Carol already had a steady boyfriend who worked in Rochester, 80 miles from Buffalo, and couldn't see her on weeknights. As soon as she was free of him for the day she would call Harry, who certainly had no pressing engagements at night.

They kept their tryst a secret through every tortuous, gleeful device they could, until one night Harry's gallbladder ruptured and he had to call an ambulance. Carol had already fixed the date of her wedding to her much-betrayed Russ, although she stalled the sending of invitations for as long as possible; even her parents were alarmed.

Harry convinced her to see a psychiatrist friend of his, who convinced her to go on with her plans to get married. The invitations finally went out. Harry attempted to abduct her, inviting her as a pretext to take a quick drive with him to nearby Lockport. Carol called her fiancé from a gas station and told him everything. Russ had been waiting for her for a few hours; he sped off to Lockport to save his girl and slay this monster. But when he got there, the monster had long quit the field. He'd gone home, and was sick for months.

In his diary he wrote, "There will never be another Carol. Life really is one great, sadistic joke."

It was torture then, but when Harry looked back on it he found it incomprehensible. Well, he thought to himself, those hundreds of women I had for only a few months, or only a night, or only a quarter of an hour: all of them, I suppose, were my wife.

About the Author

SALVATORE MUGNO (Trapani, 1962) is an essayist, novelist, translator, and chronicler of Sicilian life; his 50 books include monographs on Giovanni Falcone, Matteo Messina Denaro, the guillotine of Trapani, the commedia dell'arte mask of Don Peppe Nappa, and Sicilian immigrant poetry in Tunisia..

About the Translator

CARLO MASSIMO (b. 1990) is a translator, journalist, and poet. His translations include poetry by Pier Paolo Pasolini, Mario Scalesi, Nini De Vita, Aurélia Lassaque, and others. He lives in Washington, DC.

CROSSINGS
An Intersection of Cultures

Crossings is dedicated to the publication of Italian language literature and translations from Italian to English.

Rodolfo Di Biasio. *Wayfarers Four*. Translated by Justin Vitello. 1998. ISBN 1-88419-17-9. Vol 1.

Isabella Morra. *Canzoniere: A Bilingual Edition*. Translated by Irene Musillo Mitchell. 1998. ISBN 1-88419-18-6. Vol 2.

Nevio Spadone. *Lus*. Translated by Teresa Picarazzi. 1999. ISBN 1-88419-22-4. Vol 3.

Flavia Pankiewicz. *American Eclipses*. Translated by Peter Carravetta. Introduction by Joseph Tusiani. 1999. ISBN 1-88419-23-2. Vol 4.

Dacia Maraini. *Stowaway on Board*. Translated by Giovanna Bellesia and Victoria Offredi Poletto. 2000. ISBN 1-88419-24-0. Vol 5.

Walter Valeri, editor. *Franca Rame: Woman on Stage*. 2000. ISBN 1-88419-25-9. Vol 6.

Carmine Biagio Iannace. *The Discovery of America*. Translated by William Boelhower. 2000. ISBN 1-88419-26-7. Vol 7.

Romeo Musa da Calice. *Luna sul salice*. Translated by Adelia V. Williams. 2000. ISBN 1-88419-39-9. Vol 8.

Marco Paolini & Gabriele Vacis. *The Story of Vajont*. Translated by Thomas Simpson. 2000. ISBN 1-88419-41-0. Vol 9.

Silvio Ramat. *Sharing A Trip: Selected Poems*. Translated by Emanuel di Pasquale. 2001. ISBN 1-88419-43-7. Vol 10.

Raffaello Baldini. *Page Proof*. Edited by Daniele Benati. Translated by Adria Bernardi. 2001. ISBN 1-88419-47-X. Vol 11.

Maura Del Serra. *Infinite Present*. Translated by Emanuel di Pasquale and Michael Palma. 2002. ISBN 1-88419-52-6. Vol 12.

Dino Campana. *Canti Orfici*. Translated and Notes by Luigi Bonaffini. 2003. ISBN 1-88419-56-9. Vol 13.

Roberto Bertoldo. *The Calvary of the Cranes*. Translated by Emanuel di Pasquale. 2003. ISBN 1-88419-59-3. Vol 14.

Paolo Ruffilli. *Like It or Not*. Translated by Ruth Feldman and James Laughlin. 2007. ISBN 1-88419-75-5. Vol 15.

Giuseppe Bonaviri. *Saracen Tales*. Translated Barbara De Marco. 2006. ISBN 1-88419-76-3. Vol 16.

Leonilde Frieri Ruberto. *Such Is Life*. Translated Laura Ruberto. Introduction by Ilaria Serra. 2010. ISBN 978-1-59954-004-7. Vol 17.

Gina Lagorio. *Tosca the Cat Lady*. Translated by Martha King. 2009. ISBN 978-1-59954-002-3. Vol 18.

Marco Martinelli. *Rumore di acque*. Translated and edited by Thomas Simpson. 2014. ISBN 978-1-59954-066-5. Vol 19.

Emanuele Pettener. *A Season in Florida*. Translated by Thomas De Angelis. 2014. ISBN 978-1-59954-052-2. Vol 20.

Angelo Spina. *Il cucchiaio trafugato*. 2017. ISBN 978-1-59954-112-9. Vol 21.

Michela Zanarella. *Meditations in the Feminine*. Translated by Leanne Hoppe. 2017. ISBN 978-1-59954-110-5. Vol 22.

Francesco "Kento" Carlo. *Resistenza Rap*. Translated by Emma Gainsforth and Siân Gibby. 2017. ISBN 978-1-59954-112-9. Vol 23.

Kossi Komla-Ebri. *EMBAR-RACE-MENTS*. Translated by Marie Orton. 2019. ISBN 978-1-59954-124-2. Vol 24.

Angelo Spina. *Immagina la prossima mossa*. 2019. ISBN 978-1-59954-153-2. Vol 25.

Luigi Lo Cascio. *Othello*. Translated by Gloria Pastorino. 2020. ISBN 978-1-59954-158-7. Vol 26.

Sante Candeloro. *Puzzle*. Translated by Fred L. Gardaphe. 2020. ISBN 978-1-59954-165-5. Vol 27.

Amerigo Ruggiero. *Italians in America*. Translated by Mark Pietralunga. 2020. ISBN 978-1-59954-169-3. Vol 28.

Giuseppe Prezzolini. *The Transplants*. Translated by Fabio Girelli Carasi. 2021. ISBN 978-1-59954-137-2. Vol 29.

Silvana La Spina. *Penelope*. Translated by Anna Chiafele and Lisa Pike. 2021. ISBN 978-1-59954-172-3. Vol 30.

Marino Magliani. *A Window to Zeewijk*. Translated by Zachary Scalzo. 2021. ISBN 978-1-59954-178-5. Vol 31.

Alain Elkann. *Anita*. Translated by K.E. Bättig von Wittelsbach. 2021. ISBN 978-1-59954-170-9. Vol 32.

Luigi Fontanella. *The God of New York*. Translated by Siân E. Gibby. 2022. ISBN 978-1-59954-177-8. Vol 33.

Kossi Komla-Ebri. *Home*. Translated by Marie Orton. 2022. ISBN 978-1-59954-190-7. Vol 34.

Leopold Berman. *The Story of a Jewish Boy*. Translated by Giuliana Carugati. 2022. ISBN 978-1-59954-192-1. Vol 35.

Alain Elkann. *Nonna Carla*. Translated by K.E. Bättig von Wittelsbach. 2021. ISBN 978-1-59954-201-0. Vol 36.

Luigi Pirandello. *Man, Beast, and Virtue*. Translated by Alice Roche. 2024. ISBN 978-1-59954-205-8. Vol 37.

Maria Teresa Cometto. *Emma and the Angel of Central Park*. 2023. ISBN 978-1-59954-157-0. Vol 38.

Alain Elkann. *A Single Day*. Translated by K.E. Bättig von Wittelsbach. 2024. ISBN 978-1-59954-211-9. Vol 39.

Elisabetta Rasy. *The Indiscreet*. Translated by Siân E. Gibby. 2024. ISBN 978-1-59954-212-6. Vol 40.

Joseph Bathanti. *Sempre Fidele*. Translated by Marina Morbiducci and Darcy Di Mona. 2024. ISBN 978-1-59954-224-9. Vol 41.

Sofia Pirandello. *Animals*. Translated by Daniela Innocenti, Contextus. 2024. ISBN 978-1-59954-225-6. Vol 42.

Emanuele Pettener. *It's Saturday You Left Me and I'm So Beautiful*. Translated by Giorgio Tarchini. 2025. ISBN 978-1-59954-234-8. Vol 43.

www.ingramcontent.com/pod-product-compliance
Lightning Source LLC
Chambersburg PA
CBHW020212090426
42734CB00008B/1034